Chopard

GENÈVE

Inside ROSSO Ferrari®

The fall issue is here, and with it we celebrate the first full year of publication.

We could find no better way of doing it than dedicating this issue to the living legend . . . Juan Manuel Fangio.

Fangio was in Monterey and Laguna Seca in mid-August, and he stole the heart of everyone with his availability for several exhausting sessions of autograph signing and with a demonstration of his remarkably fresh driving ability.

He also established a record, being black-flagged when he passed both the camera truck and the pace car and then proceeded to complete a pair of laps of spirited driving. The man is eighty, and, to many of us, he doesn't look a day older than when he was the World Champion.

Brian King

The Pebble Beach Concours d'Elegance was simply overwhelming with its display of truly exceptional cars; I had a hard time keeping Gianni Rogliatti from photographing everything.

This year was my first Pebble Beach Concours. I had been afraid that the atmosphere there would have been too rarefied for a person like me who likes cars that can be aggressively driven. But I must say that I found an incredible number of genuine car enthusiasts to whom I could relate at this magnificent event. Next year I'll go again.

In this issue you will find the reproduction of two original oil paintings that Hector Luis Bergandi, renowned Argentinian artist and a long-time friend of Fangio, painted exclusively for **Rosso Ferrari**. I hope that you will cherish them as much as I enjoy looking at the originals hanging in my office.

Nancy Talarico

Giuseppe Greco
Publisher

President and Chief Executive Officer
Ferrari North America, Inc.

THE BEST THINGS IN LIFE ARE RED.

HERMÈS
PARIS

*Limited edition Eau d'Hermès flacon created by Saint-Louis Cristal
for the coronation of the Emperor of Japan, $ 5,000.*

THE SPIRIT OF COMPETITION

Front Cover: Juan Manuel Fangio
Illustration by Hector Luis Bergandi

Back Cover: The Murals of Monterey on Cannery Row
Photos by Brian King

CONTENTS

ROSSO FERRARI/FOUR
FALL 1991

ROSSO Ferrari.

THE OFFICIAL PUBLICATION OF FERRARI NORTH AMERICA

Giuseppe Greco
PUBLISHER

Ferrari North America, Inc.
250 Sylvan Avenue
Englewood Cliffs, New Jersey 07632

Designed and Published By
Hank Forssberg Inc.
Two University Plaza, Suite 208
Hackensack, New Jersey 07601

Henrik J. Forssberg
EDITOR

Nancy Talarico
CREATIVE DIRECTOR/DESIGNER

For Advertising Information Contact
Eileen Walton

Rosso Ferrari Magazine
Two University Plaza, Suite 208
Hackensack, New Jersey 07601
(201) 488-4800 • Telefax (201) 488-5487

OUR THANKS
TO EVERYONE
WHO CONTRIBUTED
EDITORIAL, GRAPHICS
AND PHOTOGRAPHY
FOR
ROSSO FERRARI/FOUR

SPECIAL THANKS

To Dr. Pier Lorenzo Costa
for the cover photograph
for Rosso Ferrari/One

To the Cannery Row Association
and the city of Monterey, California
for providing the beautiful murals
that line Cannery Row

In ***Rosso Ferrari***/Three, we included a Readership Survey Card to elicit your comments about our magazine.

Your response was overwhelming and immediate. Hundreds of cards poured in just days after the mailing of ***Rosso Ferrari***/Three. As we went to press on ***Rosso Ferrari***/Four, over 1200 cards had been received. We continue to receive as many as 40 and 50 cards at a time on a daily basis.

According to the survey results, an average of 4.5 people read ***Rosso Ferrari*** for every name on the mailing list. We also asked, "How thoroughly do you read ***Rosso Ferrari?***" and 74% of those of you who responded checked off that you read the magazine cover-to-cover. We are pleased that so many readers enjoy the editorial material and exclusive photography published in ***Rosso Ferrari.***

A total of 99% of you also indicated that you buy some or all of the products advertised in ***Rosso Ferrari.***

For those of you who have not yet returned your Readership Survey Card, it is not too late to be included in the count. We would appreciate hearing from you to give us the broadest picture possible of what you, our readers, think about ***Rosso Ferrari.***

Hank Forssberg
Editor

Rosso Ferrari is a constant challenge from a design perspective. My personal goal is to create a unique graphic look for each issue that will equal or better the previous issue.

On days when I just want to throw up my hands and "settle" for an easy solution to a graphic problem, I am reminded of the appreciative letters that ***Rosso Ferrari*** has received from many of you praising the design. Your response to ***Rosso Ferrari*** is gratifying and motivates all of us to create the best possible product.

One of the creative challenges for ***Rosso Ferrari***/Four involved the selection of a material for the pull-out poster featuring the brilliant illustrations of Fangio by Hector Luis Bergandi. This exclusive artwork deserved something rich in texture that would make the poster a lasting collectible. The canvas-like material chosen is similar to an actual artist's canvas, thus giving the poster a look of authenticity.

I hope you enjoy ***Rosso Ferrari***/Four!

Nancy Talarico
Creative Director
Designer

The Chase Manhattan Private Bank

Helping You Reach Your Financial Destination.

Chase Manhattan has a tradition of providing customized financial services to wealthy individuals based on the Chase philosophy: the long view. Our philosophy is driven by an unwavering focus on your long-term financial goals.

At Chase Manhattan, a Private Banker works directly with you to determine your needs, and together we can create a total financial plan that helps you pursue your financial objectives.

We actively manage fixed income and equity investments and can finance special purchases. Chase will tailor a comprehensive array of these and other financial services to meet your specific needs. . .because Chase knows that each individual is unique and requires special attention over a lifetime.

If you have investable assets of $1,000,000 and you want exceptional personalized service, speak to a Chase Private Banker. We have offices in New York, Connecticut, Florida, and California. Call Raymond DeRiggi or Jennifer Jahrling at (212) 789-5398, and they will put you in touch with the Chase Private Banker nearest you.

The road to your financial destination will be easier to navigate with a Chase Manhattan Private Banker by your side.

The Chase Manhattan Private Bank

Ferrari Forum

EDITOR'S NOTE

We are pleased that the Ferrari Forum section of **Rosso Ferrari** *has received such an overwhelming response from our readers. Your letters have helped us to develop future story ideas and to understand the types of articles that most interest you. We encourage you to communicate with us on a regular basis. The Ferrari Forum is* your *forum for expressing your thoughts about* **Rosso Ferrari**, *past articles, and your personal experiences as a Ferrari owner. We look forward to hearing from you!*

Enclosed is my Readership Survey Card. I could expand each of the six categories to express my views, but what I really wish to convey is: "What is not broken needs not to be fixed."

I enjoy the publication just the way it is. It would be presumptuous of me to critique the content. It is enough to receive it gratis just because I happen to own three of the finest motor cars in the world.

> William A. Lester
> Granite Bay, CA

Editor's note — *The following letter was written in response to a letter which appeared in a past Ferrari Forum.*

I read with interest the letter from James J. Viciana suggesting articles devoted to "everyday Ferrari owners." Your response that "...it is very difficult to find a common man who owns a Ferrari" is for the most part true; however, there is such a group of tifosi here in Vermont...

Our cars include a 340 America, a 250 Lusso, a GTE, a 330GT 2+2, and several 308s and Dinos. While many of these cars are unrestored, they are all very presentable and in excellent running condition. None of us are wealthy, and we all resisted the temptation of selling our treasures for the equivalent of several years' salary when the market was at its peak. Though our professions range from truck driver to architect, we all manage to maintain and enjoy our Ferraris as Mr. Ferrari intended. Depending on the season, we will be found together for rallies, track events, car shows, spaghetti dinners, and just plain cruisin'.

> Robert Weeks
> St. Albans, VT

I wish to send this note of appreciation to thank you and your staff for the terrific work of **Rosso Ferrari**/Three. As with editions One and Two, **Rosso Ferrari**/Three is simply magnificent!

I must tell you that I particularly enjoyed "That Night at Sebring" by Franco Gozzi. Since becoming a racing fan and a Ferrari enthusiast, I have been interested to learn more of the career of driver Nino Vaccarella. (I do not yet know if we are related, however I do affectionately refer to him as "Uncle Nino" in conversation). To know that he drove to victory with the likes of Mario Andretti is particularly interesting to me. I believe, too, that Nino Vaccarella won the 24 Hour race at LeMans in 1965 for the factory with co-driver Guichet and also appeared in a handful of Formula One races. I hope that in future editions you will explore Ferrari's success at LeMans, as well as "Uncle Nino's" successes with Ferrari.

Again, thank you for the excellence of **Rosso Ferrari**. I will be awaiting future issues, as well as pieces on LeMans and Nino Vaccarella, with great anticipation.

> Dr. Steven Vaccarella
> Englewood, New Jersey

I've been meaning to write since I received **Rosso Ferrari**/One. Thank you.

Having been a Ferrari owner for more than 25 years, I can say with some knowledge that **Rosso** is the best Ferrari magazine ever! So I opened **Rosso Ferrari**/Three with enthusiasm. I was thus doubly happy when I found my car (SN 538M) pictured in the magazine.

Keep up the good work!

> William H. Shaker, P.E.
> Arlington, VA

Please find enclosed my reply card for the Readership Survey of **Rosso Ferrari**. As you can see, I am highly impressed and delighted with your fine new publication.

As the owner of a Ferrari (308 GTSi, SN 35211), as well as an active enthusiast in Ferrari organizations and activities for many years, I am delighted to receive a Ferrari-related publication of high quality devoid of the intensive commercialization and aggressive marketing characteristic of the current crop of internationally-based Ferrari periodicals.

I was indeed surprised to receive the first issues of **Rosso Ferrari**, inasmuch as I have only recently relocated to New Jersey from San Francisco. Your staff deserves congratulations for their incredible job and accuracy in research with respect to maintaining records of current owners of Ferraris in the U.S.

I relate only one criticism of your publication: that it appears too infrequently! The first three issues have been read from cover-to-cover and judiciously placed in my large collection of Ferrari literature for future pleasure and reference. With respect to suggestions for **Rosso Ferrari**, I would enjoy a photo-narrative "Salon" feature in each issue highlighting a rare, unusual, or historically significant Ferrari currently owned by individuals receiving your publication. The past articles on the Ferraris of Jaeger and Lauren seemed more oriented to the owners rather than specific vehicles. Perhaps your soliciting interest and willingness from owners of such vehicles in a future issue would confirm the feasibility of such a "Salon" feature.

Nevertheless, thank you once more for the creation of the most elegant and intelligent of all Ferrari periodicals, and for remembering to include me on your mailing list.

> Stephen A. Schwartz, DMD, PhD
> Short Hills, NJ

Editor's note — *We are always interested in hearing from present owners with cars that have fascinating histories. Readers should submit detailed information about their car or cars, along with photographs. While we cannot guarantee that all such material will be used, we will carefully consider all submissions for future issues.* ❦

Riva. Beyond Comparison.

Introducing the

Limited Edition

For those who know. . .there's only one choice.
For those who take their fun seriously,
Riva is the ultimate in performance and luxury.
From Ferrari Engineering, the performance you have come to expect.
From Riva, the quality you demand.

Riva. The only choice for those who know.

For complete information call 1-800-444-RIVA

WHAT A WEEKEND! MONTEREY.

Historic Automobile Races at Laguna Seca.

A tribute to Juan Manuel Fangio.

Cars, cars and a whole lot more.

The Concours d'Elegance at Pebble Beach.

Concours Italiana at Quail Lodge, Carmel Valley.

Fangio, Ferrari and the Finest Vintage Cars.

If you are a vintage car lover and didn't spend the August 16th weekend in Monterey, California, you missed the ultimate weekend: the 1991 Concours d'Elegance at Pebble Beach; the Monterey Historic Automobile Races at Laguna Seca; the Concours Italiana in Carmel Valley and much, much more.

You missed a triple treat: the world's most impressive display of privately owned vintage cars; a special tribute to the undisputed king of racing, Juan Manuel Fangio; and the ever exciting and nostalgic Historic Automobile Races.

The Concours at Pebble Beach is truly a world class event.

The presence of Fangio made the weekend nothing short of spectacular. With as much class off the circuit as on, the eighty-year-old overachiever spent hours on Friday during the outdoor reception in his honor signing thousands of autographs for his generations of admirers.

Of course, you have to expect this sort of thing when you are the undisputed king of the racing world. Fangio began his racing career in 1936 behind the wheel of a borrowed Ford T. In 1956, he spent a season with Ferrari, winning the fourth of his record five world driving championships in a Lancia Ferrari D50. His eight-year career in Grand Prix racing stands unmatched, unparalleled and unequalled. He is simply the best of the best.

This brings us to the weekend to end all weekends. Magnificent cars. Auctions. Swap meets, literature and memorabilia. Vintage racing. The Sixth Annual Automotive Fine Arts Society Preview and show; the industry's premier automotive art exhibit. Celebrities and champions...Froilan "il cabezon" Gonzalez, Dan Gurney, Phil Hill, Jackie Stewart, Ralph Lauren, Clint Eastwood, Hector Bergandi, David E. Davis, and many, many more friends. The

The competition and judging were fierce.

A surprise visit by Fangio in the Mercedes-Benz W 196.

TUSCANY

*Evocative, lyrical, a landscape of pastel
softness infused with joyous poetry.
The ever-changing play of light on gently
undulating hills; delicate brushstrokes of fragrant
gorse and lavender. Gnarled pines,
vines and olive trees. An unassuming haven
of peace and harmony. Its mantle,
the immensity of the radiant blue sky.*

FLORENCE

*Polished jewel of the Medicis,
imbued with refined nobility
and beauty; austerity and luminous
clarity tempered by a gentle,
graceful elegance.
Source of inspiration to
Leonardo, Michelangelo, Raphael
and Galileo. Loved and admired by
Goethe and Stendhal.
A paradise of narrow lanes,
delightful cafés and bustling life.
Spiced with the allure of
seductive fashions and sparkling
exuberance. A glorious pearl nestling
in an enchanted land.*

CULTURE

*Ageless glories of a golden past.
Art and architecture to
contemplate in wonder and awe.
Vibrant, vigorous and serene:
precious blossoming of a creativity
deep-rooted in its native soil.
Man's eternal quest
for truth and beauty revealed
as a celebration of the creation.
An affirmation of life itself.*

THE
GRAND HOTEL

*The splendours of the fifteenth century
preserved to the last detail;
lovingly restored in the original Florentine style
by a team of exceptional craftsmen.
Sumptuous rooms adorned with remarkable frescoes,
each a marvel of the artists' imagination
and restorers' skill. Precious brocade,
luxurious marble baths with lovely inlaid work.
Outstanding service and superb cuisine
embracing an impressive variety of international
and local specialities.
Situated right in the heart of the city on the banks
of the Arno, opposite the Excelsior.*

HOTEL
EXCELSIOR

*Gathering place of the cream of
Florentine society; second home to Artur Rubinstein,
Erich Maria Remarque, Charlie Chaplin
and Orson Welles.
Luxurious restaurant, bar and frescoed hall
bathed in the warm radiance of
period stained glass. Dinner by starlight
above the ancient city roofs and
the shimmering Arno.
Superlative style and elegance,
just moments away from some of the world's
greatest art treasures and
most exclusive shops and stores.*

CIGA HOTELS

Austria   France   Italy   Japan   Spain   The Netherlands   United States

For information and reservations contact your travel agent or Ciga Hotels, New York, U.S.A., (212) 9359540 or toll free 1-800-221-2340

Annual Concours Italiana. Plenty of Ferrari Club activities, a special appearance by Gianni Rogliatti at the Ferrari Club of America dinner. And, of course, the presence of the honored guest, Juan Manuel Fangio.

This year's Concours d'Elegance at Pebble Beach and the Monterey Historic Races at Laguna Seca raceway were truly impressive and left us looking ahead to next year's event with great anticipation.

As much as we wanted to be everywhere and not miss a thing,

If you love Italian cars like we do, Concours Italiana was the place to be.

we quickly determined that drawing up a carefully planned itinerary would be the best course to pursue.

Friday, August 16th

We started at the 5th Annual Concours Italiana at the Quail Lodge Country Club in Carmel Valley. Here, the focus was on appreciation, not competition. We found an incredible cross-section of 300 Italian automobiles, ranging from a 1953 Maserati A6GCS to

Ferrari at Concours Italiana

Mark Allison, San Jose, CA	1978 Ferrari 308GTB
Larry Bartschi, Chico, CA	1979 Ferrari 512BB
Mark Barudoni, Folsom, CA	1983 Ferrari 308 GTSi QV
David Berelson, Jr., Incline Village, NV	1972 Ferrari 365 GTB4 Daytona
Robert Blair, San Jose, CA	1973 Ferrari 365GTB/4
Bill Boezinger, Anaheim, CA	1978 Ferrari 308 GT4
Paul Braslow, Mill Valley, CA	1987 Ferrari 328 GTS
Tom Brockmiller, Rolling Hills, East, CA	1967 Ferrari 330 GTC
Marc Burch, Los Gatos, CA	1978 Ferrari 308 GTS
Glenn Burkett, Alamo, CA	1967 Ferrari 330 GTS
Ronald Busuttil, Los Angeles, CA	1983 Ferrari 512BBi
	1977 Ferrari 308GTB
Jim Carpenter, Chandler, AZ	1978 Ferrari 308/GTO
	1979 Ferrari 308 GT4/P4
Nick Cole, San Clemente, CA	1979 Ferrari 400i
Chris Conte, Los Angeles, CA	1978 Ferrari 308 GTS Modified
Carl Corbett, Escondido, CA	1977 Ferrari 400GT
Larry Cusick, Westlake, CA	1980 Ferrari 308 GTSi
Bill DelHagen, Playa Del Ray, CA	1978 Ferrari 308 GT4
Timothy Dermody, Danville, CA	1985 Ferrari GTS QV
Skeets Dunn/Antonio Covelli,	
Rancho Sante Fe, CA	1960 Ferrari 250 GT PF Cabriolet
Bob Escalle, Solvang, CA	1978 Ferrari 308 GTS
Stephen Fouce, Green Valley, CA	1983 Ferrari Mondial QV Cape
Sal Garcia, San Francisco, CA	1984 Ferrari 512 BBi
Talman Geffs	1981 Ferrari 400i
Judd Goldfeder, Escondido, CA	1969 Ferrari 365 GTC
Gerry Guerin, Pacific Grove, CA	1985 Ferrari Testarossa
John Paul Hanna, Palo Alto, CA	1974 Ferrari 246 GTS
Hiroshi Hosobe, Sunnyvale, CA	1983 Ferrari Mondial Cabriolet
Bill Inglis, Woodland Hills, CA	1968 Ferrari 330 GTC
Bruce Jenett, Redwood City, CA	1975 Ferrari 308 GT4
Gary Kuntz, Danville, CA	1972 Ferrari 365 GTC-4
Dennis Levett, Carmel, CA	Ferrari
Doug Manista, Yorba Linda, CA	1981 Ferrari Boxer 512
Larry Miller, Woodland Hills, CA	1974 Ferrari 246 GTS "Dino"
Doug Miraco, Pebble Beach, CA	1989 Ferrari GTS
Roger Moore, Palos Verdes, CA	1986 Ferrari 328 GTB
James Moriarty, Pebble Beach, CA	1986 Ferrari Testarossa
Dave Morro, Daly City, CA	1984 Ferrari 308 GTSi
George Neuwald, Aptos, CA	1980 Ferrari 308 GT5i
James Norling, Denver, CO	1988 Ferrari Mondial Cabriolet
Ron Profili, San Francisco, CA	1984 Ferrari 308
Geoffrey Rappaport, San Francisco, CA	1973 Ferrari 246 GTS
Walter Schmidt, Sausalito, CA	1978 Ferrari 308 GTS
Marc Souza, Watsonville, CA	Ferrari
Chris Springer, Los Gatos, CA	1976 Ferrari 308 GTB
John Thayer, Santa Barbara, CA	1979 Ferrari 308 GTS
Tom Thinesen, Sunnyvale, CA	1972 Ferrari 246 GTS "Dino"
Mars Webster, Manhattan Beach, CA	1984 Ferrari 400i
James Wilkinson, Orange, CA	Ferrari
Robert Yantz, Valencia, CA	1985 Ferrari 308 GTS QV

When you drive a Ferrari, you drive one-of-a-kind.
When you wear a Brioni, you wear one-of-a-kind.

A commitment to the finest hand-tailored
men's clothing in the world.

ROMA

HAND-TAILORED IN ITALY SINCE 1945

ROMA • FIRENZE
NEW YORK
55 East 52nd St.

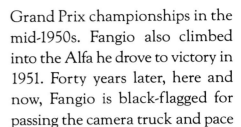

The Ferrari D50 at Laguna Seca.

The vintage car races at Laguna Seca were the main attraction of the weekend.

Grand Prix championships in the mid-1950s. Fangio also climbed into the Alfa he drove to victory in 1951. Forty years later, here and now, Fangio is black-flagged for passing the camera truck and pace car. The eighty-year-old undisputed king of race car drivers has yet to slow down!

All weekend, Ferrari Club activities were happening. We attended that evening's Ferrari Club of America dinner. It was a grand opportunity for Ferrari Club members, Ferrari senior management, and special guests to meet, mingle and talk Ferrari. The highlight of the evening was Gianni Rogliatti's informal, stirring tribute to Enzo Ferrari. The curator of the Ferrari Archives, Rogliatti shared exclusive never-before-seen photos of Mr. Ferrari while he spoke of the

the 1991 Ferrari F40 at this celebration of Italian automotive design and engineering. This year, Lamborghini was the featured marque. Also under the exhibit tent we found carloads of automobile literature and memorabilia of all kinds. Here, you could pick up just about anything relating to Ferrari.

On Friday evening we attended the outdoor reception in honor of Mr. Fangio and enjoyed meeting and socializing with the thousands of genuine car enthusiasts who came to pay tribute to Fangio. We took lots of photos and met lots of wonderful people.

Saturday, August 17th

We made our way to the Laguna Seca raceway in Monterey for the annual Historic Automobile Races and for the opportunity to watch Juan Manuel Fangio drive parade laps in the Mercedes-Benz W 196 that he piloted to two

Champion Fangio and the D50.

Elegance...best describes the Concours at Pebble Beach.

man he knew and the mystique ...that curious combination characteristic to an enduring legend known the world over. Too early, it seemed, Mr. Rogliatti's personal recollections came to a close, offering a captivated audience the chance to ask him questions.

Rather appropriately, the dinner was also an occasion to honor Giuseppe Greco with a special award presented by the Ferrari Club of America's Pacific Region in appreciation of Mr. Greco having established a better communications network between three Ferrari entities: Ferrari Club owners/members, Ferrari owners throughout North America, and the Ferrari factory, largely through the work of **Rosso Ferrari.** Linking two coasts and two continents together is no small feat. It is a much deserved award for Mr. Greco.

Sunday, August 18th

Next on our itinerary was the 41st Annual Pebble Beach Concours d'Elegance, held on the kelly green lawn of The Lodge at Pebble Beach, overlooking the 18th green of the legendary Pebble Beach Golf Links. Of course, one might have expected to see Bob Hope near a golf course... but other celebrities turned out as well. The biggest surprise, however, was an unannounced and unpublicized appearance by Fangio, who drove up in the Mercedes-Benz W 196 to kick off the awards ceremony.

As always, the real stars of the Concours d'Elegance are the automobiles. This premier event continues to attract the rarest of clas-

The trophies were beautiful.

Dan Gurney

Froilan "il cabezon" Gonzalez.

The Ferrari models shown at Pebble Beach were exquisite.

sic cars from around the world, some of which date back to the turn of the century. If your heart belongs to vintage cars, if it beats a little faster at the sight of a 1959 Ferrari 250GT TDF or a 1956 Corvette or a 1923 Bugatti 32, then it got quite a workout savoring the world's most impressive display of privately owned vintage cars.

Over the years, the Concours d'Elegance has evolved from an informal regional event to a formal world class event that draws only the most accomplished entrants and judges from around the world.

Changes occurred slowly, but meaningfully. It was in the 1960s that special classes of cars were established. It was also during this time that automobiles of similar background or heritage were judged on a specific merit objective basis. Unlike the decade before, score cards and a point system were adopted.

In the early 1970s, the Concours got a needed jump start from Lorin Tryon and Jules Heumann who established more specific marque classes. And it was in the 1980s that the Concours really came into its own as the premier quintessential vintage car show.

This year's Concours d'Elegance bestowed awards in eighteen categories including **Best of Show, Ansel Adams Memorial Trophy,** and the **French Cup,** as well as the Class Awards. Featured marques were **Rolls-Royce, Pierce-Arrow** and a special exhibition of **American Dream Cars.** As always, the Concours brings out the best of the best in the history of vintage motor cars.

For all of us who love motorcars, especially vintage cars, this was the weekend to end all weekends. This was everything you always dreamed about and more than you could imagine. Make your plans early, because next year's events promise to be even more magnificent. 🐎

See you next August in Monterey!

The Ferrari Club of America Dinner. Gianni Rogliatti's talk was inspirational. He showed many never-before-seen photos of Enzo Ferrari.

Bill Schworer, President of Ferrari Club, Pacific Region, presented Mr. Greco with the FCA Award of Appreciation.

Battaglia

BATTAGLIA BABY CALF
SKIN LEATHER JACKETS IN ROYAL BLUE
AND FERRARI RED. ABOUT $4500.
EXQUISITELY SOFT.
BATTAGLIA, BEVERLY HILLS.
306 NORTH RODEO DRIVE
(213) 276-7184

THE BEST OF BRIONI . STEFANO RICCI . ARTIOLI . ZILLI. BATTAGLIA, BEVERLY HILLS

1932 Chrysler CH LeBaron Speedster.

1991 Pebble Beach Concours d'Elegance
Class Winners 1st, 2nd & 3rd

Class A (Antique through 1915)
Joel Naive, Bigfork, MT — 1908 Mercedes 45HP 7 Passenger Touring
Raymond H. Miller, Kalamazoo, MI — 1911 Daimler 6/23 5 Passenger Tourer
Robert & Linda Sohl, Santa Cruz, CA — 1915 Mercer 22-70 Sporting

Class C-1 (American Classic 1925-1932 Open)
Sam & Emily Mann, Englewood, NJ — 1932 Chrysler CH LeBaron Speedster
J. Brent McKinley, Arlington, WA — 1932 Auburn 8-100A Boattail Speedster
Noel Thompson, New Vernon, NJ — 1932 Stutz DV-32 Rollston Convertible Coupe

Class C-2 (Packard 1925-1932 Open)
Robert E. Turnquist, Morristown, NJ — 1931 Packard 840 Roadster
Ken & Marjorie Metzger, Belvedere, CA — 1931 Packard 840 Convertible Coupe
Imperial Palace Auto Collection, Las Vegas, NV — 1932 Packard 904 Dietrich Convertible Victoria

Class C-3 (American Classic 1925-1941 Closed)
Jacques Harguindeguy, Walnut Creek, CA — 1930 Stutz MB Weymann Monte Carlo
J.B. Nethercutt, Sylmar, CA — 1930 Packard 734 Speedster Victoria
Benson Ford, Jr., Dearborn, MI — 1929 Lincoln L LeBaron Opera Coupe

Class D-1 (American Classic 1933-1941 Open)
Joseph B. Folladori, Indianapolis, IN — 1934 Auburn 1250 Salon Phaeton
Dr. Barbara Atwood, Rockford, IL — 1934 Auburn 1250 Salon Phaeton
Terry Radey, Etobicoke, Ontario, Canada — 1940 Cadillac 62 Bohman & Schwartz Convertible Coupe

Class D-2 (Packard 1933-1941 Open)
William Buddig, Frankfort, IL — 1934 Packard 1107 Phaeton
Vic & Cecilia Nelson, Palo Alto, CA — 1933 Packard 1005 Coupe-Roadster
Bob & Jo Zaitlin, Los Angeles, CA — 1933 Packard 1004 Coupe-Roadster

Class E (American Classic 16 Cylinders 1930-1937)
Dr. Barbara Atwood, Rockford, IL — 1935 Cadillac 452D Fleetwood Convertible Sedan
Fred W. Weber, St. Louis, MO — 1930 Cadillac 452 Saoutchik Berline
Elliott & Katherine Klein, Paradise Valley, CA — 1931 Cadillac 452A Fleetwood All Weather Phaeton

Class F (European and American Classic New Coachwork)
Fran Roxas, Alsip, IL — 1934 Packard 1108 LeBaron-Style Sport Phaeton
Donald E. Zerth, Lansing, IL — 1929 Duesenberg LaGrande-Style Dual Cowl Phaeton
Jack A. Goffette, Lynnwood, WA — 1928 Bugatti Type 44 Roadster

Class G (Duesenberg)
William R. Patton, Newport Beach, CA — 1935 Duesenberg J Rollston Torpedo Victoria
Imperial Palace Auto Collection, Las Vegas, NV — 1934 Duesenberg J Fernandez et Darrin Cabriolet
Michael J. Calore, Exeter, RI — 1934 Duesenberg LeBaron Convertible Berline

Class H-1 (Rolls-Royce Silver Ghost, Early)
Robert M. Lee, Reno, NV — 1907 Rolls-Royce Silver Ghost 7 Passenger Tourer
Robert M. Lee, Reno, NV — 1912 Rolls-Royce Silver Ghost London to Edinburgh Holmes Torpedo
Millard Newman, Tampa, FL — 1907 Rolls-Royce Silver Ghost Rippon Brothers Limousine

Class H-2 (Rolls-Royce Large Horsepower)
Frank & Jan Hamilton, Reno, NV — 1921 Rolls-Royce Silver Ghost Brockman Speedster
Rodney D. Adams, Tucson, AZ — 1932 Rolls-Royce Phantom II Brewster Henley
Virgil Millett, Huntington, NY — 1936 Rolls-Royce Phantom III Cooper Tourer

Class I (European Classic 1925-1939)
John Mozart, Palo Alto, CA — 1935 Hispano-Suiza J12 VanVooren Cabriolet
Noel Thompson, New Vernon, NJ — 1934 Delage D8-SS Fernandez et Darrin Cabriolet
Blackhawk Collection, Danville, CA — 1931 Isotta Fraschini 8A Castagna Landaulet

1959 Ferrari Testa Rossa Fantuzzi Spyder.

1991 Pebble Beach Concours d'Elegance
Specialty Awards

Award	Recipient
Automobile Quarterly Trophy	Millard Newman, Tampa FL 1907 Rolls-Royce Silver Ghost Rippon Brothers Limousine
Road & Track Trophy	Arlan Ettinger, Tuxedo Park, NY 1953 Maserati A6GCS Fantuzzi Racer
Hans Tanner Memorial Trophy	G.C. Pete Lovely, Tacoma, WA 1959 Ferrari 250 Testa Rossa Fantuzzi Spyder
Mercedes-Benz Trophy	Joel Naive, Bigfork, MT 1908 Mercedes 45HP 7 Passenger Touring
Alec Ulmann Memorial Trophy	John Mozart, Palo Alto, CA 1935 Hispano-Suiza J12 VanVooren Cabriolet
Charles A. Chayne Memorial Trophy	Blackhawk Collection, Danville, CA 1931 Isotta Fraschini 8A Castagna Landaulet
Montagu of Beaulieu Trophy	Raymond H. Miller, Kalamazoo, MI 1911 Daimler 6/23 5 Passenger Tourer
Lucius Beebe Memorial Trophy	Charles B. Gillet, Baltimore, MD 1926 Rolls-Royce Phantom I Barker Salamanca
The French Cup	Gary Wales, Woodland Hills, CA 1947 Bentley MK VI Franay Cabriolet
Ansel Adams Memorial Trophy	National Automobile Museum, Reno, NV 1913 Pierce-Arrow 66 7 Passenger Touring
Briggs Cunningham Trophy	Richard DeLuna, San Mateo, CA 1912 Hudson Mile-A-Minute Roadster
The Pebble Beach Cup	Robert Rubin, Paris, France 1929 Miller Racer

Gwenn Graham Memorial Trophies:

Most Elegant Open Car	Jerome Sauls, Springfield, PA 1933 Packard 1006 Dietrich Sport Phaeton
Most Elegant Closed Car	Robert F. Goodwin, Hayward, CA 1932 Rolls-Royce Phantom II Brewster Sports Sedan
Most Elegant Convertible Car	Jim Friswold, Portland, OR 1935 Mercedes-Benz 500K H.J. Mulliner Drophead
Co-Chairman's Trophy	Brenda and Skip Berg, Tiburon, CA 1931 Bugatti Type 54 O-Uhlik Roadster
Best of Show	**Sam and Emily Mann, Englewood, NJ 1932 Chrysler CH LeBaron Speedster**

Class J (European Sports and Racing 1925-1939)
John Ridings Lee, Dallas, TX — 1930 Alfa Romeo 6C 1750 Zagato Gran Sport Spyder
Brenda & Skip Berg, Tiburon, CA — 1931 Bugatti Type 54 O-Uhlik Roadster
R. Stuart Bewley, Belvedere, CA — 1939 Talbot-Lago 150CSS Pourtout Aerodynamic Coupe

Class K (European Custom Coachwork, Postwar)
Gary Wales, Woodland Hills, CA — 1947 Bentley MK V1 Franay Cabriolet
Blackhawk Collection, Danville, CA — 1949 Delahaye 178 Saoutchik Cabriolet

Class L (Dream Cars)
Not Judged

Class M (Ferrari, Custom Coachwork through 1964)
G.C. Pete Lovely, Tacoma, WA — 1959 Ferrari 250 Testa Rossa Fantuzzi Spyder
Eleanore Haga, Westlake Village, CA — 1950 Ferrari 166MM Touring Barchetta
C.A. Dunn, Rancho Santa Fe, CA — 1960 Ferrari 250GT Pininfarina Cabriolet Series II

Class N-1 (Italian Custom Coachwork 1946-1956)
David B. Smith, Bellevue, WA — 1955 Lancia B24S Pinin Farina Spyder
Arlan Ettinger, Tuxedo Park, NY — 1953 Maserati A6GCS Fantuzzi Racer
Kaid Marouf, La Jolla, CA — 1955 Alfa Romeo 1900 Sprint Zagato Coupe

Class N-2 (Italian Custom Coachwork 1957-1967)
Norb McNamara, Waterford, CA — 1963 ATS 2500 GT Allemano Coupe
Steven Nanny, Encino, CA — 1967 DeTomaso Ghia Mangusta Spyder
Kaid Marouf, La Jolla, CA — 1965 Alfa Romeo TZ 2 Zagato Coupe

Class O (SIATA)
Scott Borman, Los Angeles, CA — 1953 SIATA 208 S Michelotti Spyder
Harry & Anita Hart, Belmont, CA — 1951 SIATA 1400 Gran Sport Stablimenti Farina Spyder
Court Whitlock, Springfield, MO — 1953 SIATA 200 CS Bertone Spyder

Class P-1 (Mercedes-Benz 1925-1934)
Paul Karassik, Monsey, NY — 1934 Mercedes-Benz 500K Cabriolet A
Imperial Palace Auto Collection, Las Vegas, NV — 1930 Mercedes-Benz 770K Castagna Cabriolet
Dale A. Lyons, Dowagiac, MI — 1927 Mercedes-Benz K Sport Touring

Class P-2 (Mercedes-Benz 1935-1939)
Fred Kriz, Los Angeles, CA — 1937 Mercedes-Benz 540K Special Coupe
Jim Friswold, Portland, OR — 1935 Mercedes-Benz 500K H.J. Mulliner Drophead
R.H. Wesselink, San Juan Capistrano, CA — 1939 Mercedes-Benz 540K Roadster

Class R-1 (Pierce-Arrow through 1920)
Rick Rawlins, South Laguna, CA — 1913 Pierce-Arrow 38 Suburban
J.B. Nethercutt, Sylmar, CA — 1910 Pierce-Arrow 48 7 Passenger Touring
Robert J. Gottlieb, Beverly Hills, CA — 1914 Pierce-Arrow 38 Suburban

Class R-2 (Pierce-Arrow 1921-1938)
Gerald E. Schimke, Seattle, WA — 1932 Pierce-Arrow 52 Club Berline
Mary & Al Zamba, Pittsburgh, PA — 1933 Pierce-Arrow 1247 LeBaron Convertible Sedan
Roy I. Warshawsky, Chicago, IL — 1936 Pierce-Arrow 1603 Derham Town Car

A Decade of the Finest
Concours d'Elegance Best of Show Winners

Year Owners	Best of Show
1991—Sam & Emily Mann, Englewood, NJ	1932 Chrysler CH LeBaron Speedster
1990—Ralph Lauren, New York, NY	1938 Bugatti 57SC Atlantic
1989—Robert L. Meyer, King City, CA	1922 Hispano-Suiza H6B Labourdette Skiff
1988—Mr. & Mrs. John Mozart, Palo Alto, CA	1937 Alfa Romeo 2900B Touring Spyder
1987—Thomas Lester, Deerfield Beach, FL	1928 Minerva AF Ostruk Berline Transformable
1986—Arturo Keller, Tiburon, CA	1936 Mercedes-Benz 540K Special Roadster
1985—Jack Becronis, San Marino, CA	1939 Bugatti Type 57 Saoutchik Cabriolet
1984—Mr. & Mrs. Kenneth Vaughn, Coeur d'Alene, ID	1929 Cunningham V5410 Allweather Cabriolet
1983—Dr. Irwin Ginsberg, Buffalo, NY	1930 Isotta Fraschini Tipo 8ASS Castagna Special Sports Tourer
1982—Mr. & Mrs. Tom Perkins, Belvedere, CA	1935 Mercedes-Benz 500K Special Roadster
1981—Terry Radey, Islington, Ontario, Canada	1929 Dusenberg J Murphy Convertible Coupe

Ferrari at Pebble Beach

G.C. Pete Lovely, Tacoma, WA	250 Testa Rossa Fantuzzi Spyder
Eleanore Haga, Westlake Village, CA	166 MM Touring Barchetta
C.A. Dunn, Rancho Santa Fe, CA	250 GT PF Cabriolet Series II
Castello Family, San Jose, CA	500 Testa Rossa Scaglietti Spyder
Greg Garrison, Thousand Oaks, CA	410 SA PF Speciale "Superfast"
Anthony Wang, Lloyd Harbor, NY	250 GT LWB Spyder California
Gordon Wheeler, Amgwin, CA	212 Inter Vignale Coupe

Sam and Emily Mann of Englewood, New Jersey are the proud owners of the Best of Show.

Juan Manuel Fangio

FIVE TIME WORLD DRIVING CHAMPION

*Fangio drives to victory in the
1956 British Grand Prix.*

Photography by Geoffrey Goddard

1956 French Grand Prix.

1956 British Grand Prix.

1956 Monaco Grand Prix.

1956 British Grand Prix.

1956 French Grand Prix.

1956 French Grand Prix.
In the Ferrari garage, pilots Collins, Gendebien, De Portago, Fangio and Castellotti.

1956 French Grand Prix.

1956 Belgian Grand Prix.

1956 French Grand Prix. Pilots Fangio, Castellotti and Collins set the pace.

JUAN MANUEL FANGIO — HIS LIFE

June 24, 1911	*Born in Balcarce, 300 kilometers south of Buenos Aires*
1923	*Fangio leaves school after cutting short obligatory school attendance*
1924	*Trained as a car mechanic*
1932	*Conscripted into military service*
1936	*First race in borrowed Ford T in Buenos Aires*
1940	*First victory with an old Chevrolet TC in the "Gran Premio International del Norte"*
1946	*Several races in a self-constructed car*
1949	*Fangio sets up as an automobile dealer*
1950	*Entry into the Alfa Romeo racing team*
1951	*World Champion with Alfa Romeo*
1952	*Serious accident in Monza*
1953	*Returned to the world of motor sport*
1954	*Entry into the Daimler-Benz AG racing team and World Champion in the Mercedes W 196*
1955	*World Champion in the Mercedes W 196*
1956	*World Champion with Ferrari*
1957	*World Champion with Maserati*
1958	*Fangio retires from the world of racing*
1974	*President of Mercedes-Benz Argentina S.A.*
1986	*The Fangio Museum is opened*
1991	*Fangio tribute at Monterey Historic Automobile Races*
Today	*Mercedes dealer, Honorary President of the Juan Manuel Fangio Foundation, potato farmer, Honorary President and Member of the Automobile Club of Argentina, of the Road Racing Association, and of Old Grand Prix Pilots*

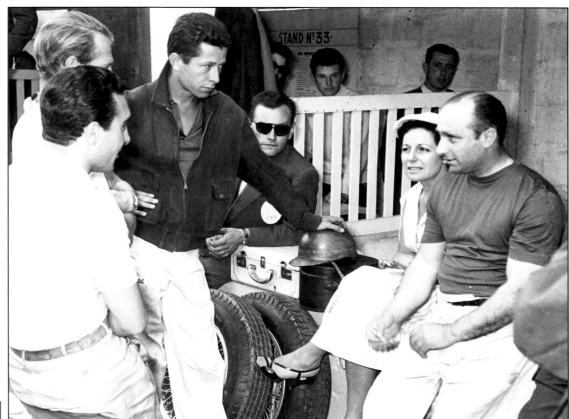

1956 French Grand Prix. The younger pilots wanted to learn from the "maestro."

1956 Monaco Grand Prix.

Ferraristi

Charles M. Jordan, Vice President of Design for General Motors, introducing David Cummins to Sergio Pininfarina during the "Eyes on the Classics" weekend.

Owner:
David Cummins

State of Residence:
Michigan

Occupation:
Design consultant on the restoration of vintage race cars. Retired from a career spanning more than 32 years in a variety of styling and engineering executive positions for Chrysler Motors.

First Introduction to Ferrari:
"I've lived, eaten and slept cars since the tender age of three. But it wasn't until I attended the Art Center School in Los Angeles (now the Art Center School of Design in Pasadena) that I saw my first Ferrari: a two-tone grey Europa on the Sunset Strip. It made rippling sounds as it went up and down the Strip. I stood there with my mouth hanging open."

Models in Collection:
410 Superamerica (serial #1495 S/A)
275 GTB/4 (serial #10329)
365 GTB/4 (serial #15281)
512 BB (serial #26947)

The 410 Superamerica Series III owned by David Cummins is one of the last Lampredi-engined Ferrari-built cars.

Most Memorable Ferrari Experience:

Buying the 275 GTB/4 in Brussels, Belgium at Jacques Swaters' Ecurie Francorchamps Dealership, one of the oldest Ferrari dealerships in existence.

Favorite Ferrari:

"You can't grade superlatives. They all have different areas of appeal."

Personal Philosophy on Ferrari Ownership:

"Maintain them properly and drive them. Ferraris should not be glass case show cars."

Why He Is a Ferrarista:

"The evidence speaks for itself. As far as I'm concerned, there's only one make of car. I first owned Jaguars, but once I learned what Ferrari was all about, the only cars I've bought since are Ferraris."

What Makes His Ferrari Collection Unique:

"That it's mine. Nothing is unique about it, except that I enjoy driving the cars and owning them."

What Car Would He Most Like to Add to the Collection:

An early open race car.

Other Hobbies/Interests:

"None really. Ferrari is an all-consuming passion."

David Cummins' cars are the epitome of perfection, obviously a reflection of his automotive design background.

The 365 GTB/4 was not available to be photographed.

Of his 512 BB, Cummins says, "This car is about as close as you can come to a streetable and tractable race car... instant response to any demand made on it!"

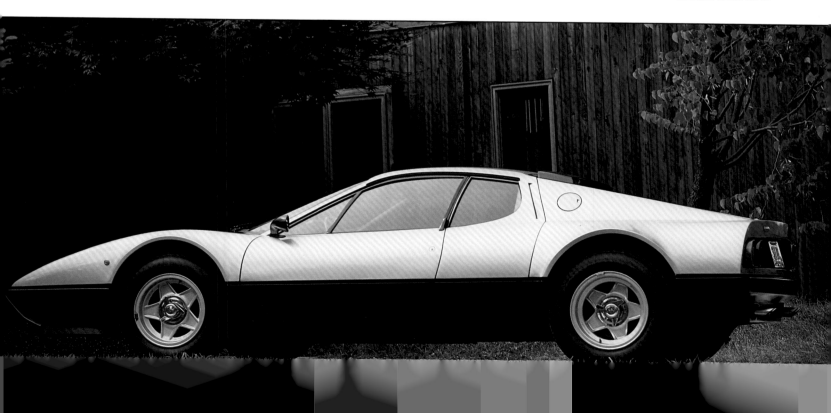

Enzo Ferrari in his sparsely furnished office at the factory. The telephone is famous because each button connected him with one of his closest associates, and woe on him who did not answer immediately!

MY FERRARI

Chapter Two

by Gianni Rogliatti

Over the years, Enzo Ferrari developed such a fine sensitivity in dealing with people that he could tune his attitude to the visitor's personality and behavior. I don't know how he was in his younger years, for I got in touch with him when he was already 58 and obviously at the top of his possibilities and with all that experience behind him. So for the period before, I must rely on the information provided by his friends and associates, many of whom I have known for a very long time, so the reports are not hearsay, but genuine pieces of a fascinating personality.

Notwithstanding the fact that a fair number of books and thousands of articles have been written about Ferrari and his machines, there are still people who do not have a clear picture of what Enzo Ferrari did before becoming a motorcar manufacturer at the age of 49 (or should we say at 42 if we take into consideration the production of the two Auto Avio Costruzioni type 815 Spyders that raced in the 1940 Mille Miglia).

Even before Enzo Ferrari became a motorcar manufacturer, he was a successful manager and a self-made man. After an honorable discharge at the end of World War I, he became a test driver — first for a small firm and then for Alfa Romeo. At 23, he was already a team driver for the Milanese firm, then at 26 sales representative for the region of Emilia Romagna, and at 31 he invented the "Scuderia Ferrari."

In 1929, the Scuderia was something unheard of: a specialized organization to allow gentlemen drivers to just enjoy racing while the Scuderia took care of everything else, from preparing the cars to looking after all paperwork concerned with the sporting activity. From there, Ferrari gra-

duated into choosing his own drivers, while improving the technical side of the activity to the point of building some cars out of Alfa Romeo parts.

In the Sixties, when faced with the success of the British teams that assembled racing cars using proprietary components, he was asked by some journalists why he did not do something like that. Ferrari snapped back, *"I did it first in the Thirties with the Bimotore*

and the Alfetta." It was true: the Bimotore was a very unusual car they tried against the overpowering German team. Lacking an engine bigger than the Alfa Romeo B type of 3165 cc and 265 hp, Ferrari, Bazzi, and company bolted two engines to the same gearbox, one ahead and one behind the driver. It was not the answer, but in 1935 they secured a speed record in the deal.

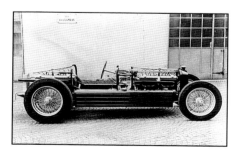

The inner workings of the Bimotore show how cleverly they put the second engine in the tail and built two long side tanks for the fuel.

The Alfa Bimotore with a group of notables: from left, a mechanic named Jotti; a young Nello Ugolini; Enzo Ferrari; Del Drogo; Luigi Bazzi; Count Trossi; Chieregato; Louis Chiron all Scuderia drivers; Saracco Ferrari, a relative of Enzo; Nuvolari; Dreyfus; Brivio; Marinoni plus two more not recognizable.

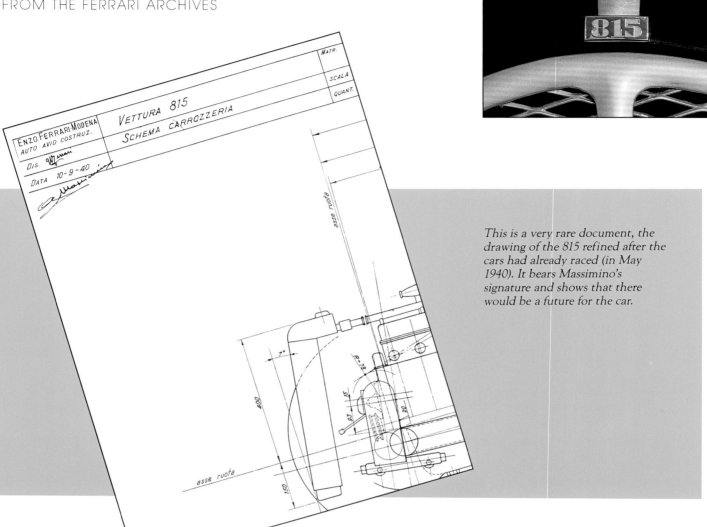

This is a very rare document, the drawing of the 815 refined after the cars had already raced (in May 1940). It bears Massimino's signature and shows that there would be a future for the car.

As for the Alfetta, it was designed and built from scraps in Modena by the Scuderia. Ferrari engineers had to work very hard to develop a design that was capable of defeating the Alfetta. On July 14, 1951, Froilan "Il Cabezon" Gonzalez deafeated the Alfa team at the British Grand Prix in a Ferrari 375 F1 (12 cyl. 380 hp).

The success of the Alfetta 158 in its early days was a sign of the good organization of the Scuderia. As a final step, Alfa Romeo bought it from Ferrari reportedly for a princely sum and retained him as its manager for an equally princely yearly fee. He was only 41.

From a financial point of view, he could have retired in his country house (the one near the Maranello factory) and just amused himself with some activity. Not him. Enzo Ferrari, true to the famous Kipling poem "If you could make a heap of all your winnings and risk them in one turn of pitch and toss" took what was possibly the biggest risk of them all — making racing cars, a choice where many others had lost their shirts.

And so the 815 came into being. Later in life he would dismiss the entire operation as just a sort of favor he did for his friends Lotario Ranqoni Machiavelli and Alberto Ascari: two cars to race in the Mille Miglia. Judging from documents that have been discovered, this was a much more sophisticated project.

First of all there was the advertising folder: a bunch of these have been found among old leftovers and clearly cast light on the fact that if you print a sales folder you plan to build and sell more cars than just the two made for friends. The second fact was that the two cars were not absolutely alike, but rather had differences that pointed to the idea of having a grand touring car (Ranqoni's car had a better finish, full upholstering, etc.) and a pure sports car (the Ascari one had a spartan interior). The Ascari car is the one that has survived, saved from destruction

in 1965 and kept under the same roof ever since. Our thanks to the owners for allowing us to photograph the car.

No question, therefore, exists about the genuineness of this car as has sometimes been suggested. I saw the car then in total abandon when nobody ever wanted it and met the man who bought it for

some $150.00! The car has been fully restored now, put in running condition, and will be preserved as the Ferrari called Auto Avio Costruzioni. This is the name that Enzo Ferrari chose for the Company during the period of four years when, according to the deal with Alfa Romeo, he could not use his own name on cars.

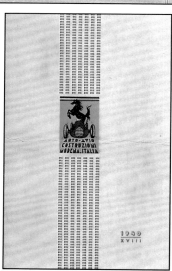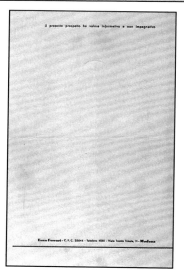

Center pages of the 815 sales brochure.

Front cover of the 815 sales brochure.

Rear cover of the 815 sales brochure.

There is more evidence to the plan for a real, if limited, production. Alberto Massimino, who did the project for this car, made sketches for a whole range of models. Apart from the 1500 cc car with a 2.42 meter wheelbase, he also designed a longer wheelbase chassis for a touring model (wheelbase 2.80) dated September 10, 1940, and a smaller 1100 cc model called the 811, with a shorter (2.350 meters) wheelbase dated April 12, 1941. On top of that, Carrozzeria Touring also designed a Cabriolet, probably destined to the long wheelbase chassis.

How, in the long war years, Ferrari and his team (Massimino, Colombo, and Bazzi, the men who made the Alfetta) worked their way from the straight eight to the V-12 is open to speculation. The fact is that they were ready as soon as the war was over. The basic 815 chassis with some modifications would become the 125 chassis, and the engine was designed by Gioachino Colombo in 1946, put to the test bench by Giuseppe Busso in the winter, and the whole car ready by the spring of 1947.

Because they were the designers and builders of the Alfetta, the Ferrari technicians knew all of its virtues and probably also its shortcomings. For example, the inline 8 engine had a long stroke that would make an increase in speed more difficult. It is a tribute to the Ferrari technicians who designed it and to the Alfa Romeo engineers who developed it to go on winning up to 1951 with a car designed in 1938.

The V-12 arrangement was chosen not only for sentimental reasons as Ferrari often said (the sound of it; the American marvel of the Packard), but for very solid technical purposes, such as the lower average piston speed and the possibility of increasing the engine capacity. Talking with Chinetti recently, we heard that he, too, suggested the V-12 choice, because of the lower stress on the engine parts. And Luigi Chinetti deserves a place in the history of sports cars, not only because he won Le Mans and imported the Ferrari to the USA, but also because he is one of the best tuners around.

The 815 shortly after having been saved from the wrecker's torch.

815, fully restored today, is the property of Messrs. Domenico Gentili and Mario Righini who kindly allowed it to be photographed.

A curious Enzo Ferrari in the Mercedes pits at the Coppa Acerbo of 1934 looks over the competitor's organization and maybe thinks of future moves. Car No. 28 was that of the eventual winner, Luigi Fagioli.

No wonder that the new Ferrari car, when announced in 1947, would catch the attention of every car enthusiast. I was living in Argentina then, was 18 and read eagerly all the car magazines I could lay my hands on. One of these magazines was **Motor Italia**, and it ran a lengthy article on the new Ferrari car. That was my first contact with the name of the marque.

I got in touch with the real McCoy in January 1949 when Nino Farina, momentarily off-duty with Alfa Romeo, arrived to dispute the Argentine "Temporada" (a set of four races) with a 125 type Monoposto equipped with a supercharged 166 engine. The races were held for the "Formula libre" meaning that anything with an engine and four wheels could compete. It is unforgettable that first acquaintance with mechanics Storchi and Salvarani, who comprised the entire Ferrari delegation. The equipment consisted of some boxes with tools and spares. The idea of changing the engine between testing sessions was something that bordered on lunacy then, and in fact Farina disputed all four races with the same engine and won once. Just compare that with what we are used to seeing today in terms of semi-trailers, vans, telemetry, and engines that last a test session.

The mechanics were only too happy to have a young and earnest enthusiast around who also spoke Spanish. So I was soon entrusted with the important task of going to the fuel storage area proudly equipped with gas cans and a piece of paper with the fuel formula to be mixed for the car. Supercharged cars of the era would use a mixture of methanol (around 85%) with benzene, acetone, and ether suitably added and a spot of castor oil to lubricate the Roots supercharger vanes. So there I was at 20, working for the Ferrari team, albeit unpaid. But who cared at the time?

As the chances of life go, I would later buy **Motor Italia** magazine (which I still own), and it was through the magazine that I would get to fulfill my lifelong dream: writing a full **Ferrari Story**. Being a journalist, I was

A young Rogliatti with a Ferrari car in Buenos Aires, January 1949; the mechanic's name is Cornelio Storchi.

impressed by the amount of work the Ferrari Company would invest in building race cars for practically every class or category. So I started to assemble tables of models, writing to Ferrari for missing details as soon as I got in contact after our famous exchange of letters.

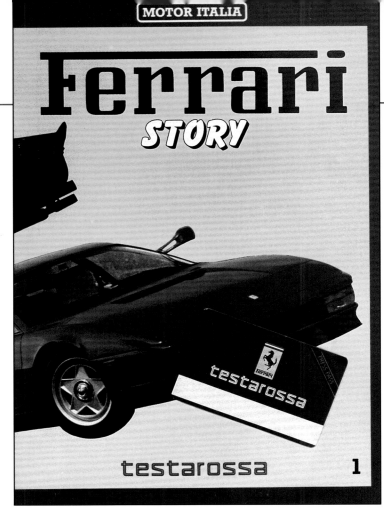

*Cover of the first issue of **Ferrari Story** magazine with invitation card No. 0001 (unused because he didn't go to the reception). The Testarossa script was transferred from card to magazine, at the suggestion of Mr. Ferrari.*

And as early as 1961, I was eager to do a book on the matter, something that Mr. Ferrari didn't like at the time. Maybe he felt his Company story was too short to be taken seriously; maybe he thought I was not mature enough for the job. The fact is that he did not allow me to write an "official story," although I did it first as a series of articles in a magazine and later as a book.

There were mistakes to be sure, and some information was missing, as was the case with most of the works on Ferrari because of the secrecy that had shrouded this Company.

Only much later, November 1984 to be exact, did he allow me to start the real **Ferrari Story** as a supplement to the magazine **Motor Italia**. It was November I recall, and I decided to try my luck once more. A supplement to **Motor Italia** was prepared bearing the title **Ferrari Story,** containing a detailed article on the new Testarossa, the car that had been launched at the Paris Motor Show.

I went to see Mr. Ferrari with the layout of the magazine like a boy going to a major examination and told him, "Well, Mr. Ferrari, I thought that maybe it was just time to start that **Ferrari Story.**"

He went slowly through those first 16 pages, looked again at the cover where the old 250 TR and the new Testarossa were shown together, and of all things pointed at the magazine's subhead "Testarossa" that was printed in a standard type.

He told me, *"The new Testarossa has a particular lettering to its name. Why don't you use it? It's nicer."* Then he took his own invitation to the Paris reception for the launching of the car and gave it to me saying, *"Give this card to your printers so they can copy the name Testarossa on the magazine cover."* Obviously, I still have that card which bears No. 1 on it.

Ferrari Story later evolved into an independent magazine which continues to be published today as a quarterly. It is small, only 32 pages, but it carries no advertising and every issue is a complete chapter of the story, with much previously unpublished information. Enzo Ferrari liked it that way and often sent me a note of approval when he received a new issue. I like it that way, too.

...to be continued

The Perfect Companion

To Your Collection
of *Rosso Ferrari* Magazines
Exclusively for our Owners and Friends

Due to the tremendous response to our offer in Rosso Ferrari/Three for the handcrafted magazine holder, we are extending the deadline for orders on this collectible item to accommodate numerous requests which arrived late.

Mauro Schedoni, famous for his handcrafted leather creations for Ferrari, has agreed to custom design an additional quantity of these elegant leather magazine holders for a limited time. The holder stores and protects the first five issues of **Rosso Ferrari**.

Crafted from the finest leather with an oak finished outer wooden encasement, *each magazine holder will be hand made as orders are received.*

A Schedoni leather book

marker, monogrammed with your initials, will be included at no additional charge.

This custom designed masterpiece is available for $110.00.

Be sure to include the initials you wish to have monogrammed on the leather book marker. Orders must be received no later than October 25th. Please allow 10-12 weeks for delivery.

Price includes handling and shipping. Add $10.00 for shipments to Canada. N.J. residents add 7% sales tax. Send check or money order payable to: Ferrari North America, Inc. *% Rosso Ferrari* magazine, Two University Plaza, Suite 208, Hackensack, N.J. 07601.

Ferrari®

·1·9·9·1·
Eyes On The Classics

HONORS

Sergio PININFARINA

It has been called the world's premier showcase of automotive design and designers. After all, it is the only place that brings together past, present and future automotive designers — and their creations — in what has become a unique and glamorous tribute to automotive design as an art form. It's called "Eyes on the Classics", and it happens only once a year.

This year, more than 200 cars — from classics to concepts — were on display at the two-day fundraiser, but the notable event-within-the-event had a more international flavor: the honoring of Sergio Pininfarina with a retro-

Charles M. Jordan, vice president of design for General Motors, presents the coveted Lifetime Automotive Design Achievement Award to Sergio Pininfarina at the "Eyes on the Classics" black tie gala.
(Photo courtesy of GM Design)

spective and a special Lifetime Automotive Design Achievement Award. It was a fitting tribute to Pininfarina. Others who have previously received the award include: Eugene T. "Bob" Gregorie (1990); Virgil M. Exner (1990); Strother Mac-Minn (1989); William Mitchell (1989); and Gordon Buehrig (1988).

Some of Pininfarina's most inspired work was on display at the 1991 "Eyes on the Classics" — including a **1953 Ferrari 375 America Berlinetta**, a **1963 Ferrari 250 GT Lusso Berlinetta**, a **1972 Ferrari 365 GTB/4 Daytona Berlinetta**, and a **1991 Ferrari F40 Berlinetta**.

While "Eyes on the Classics" is one of the premier social events of the season, it is always a huge philanthropic success. It was established in 1988 to raise funds for the Detroit Institute of Ophthalmology (DIO), a non-profit organization dedicated to ophthalmologic research, medicine and education. The DIO also offers support to the blind and the visually impaired. All this is possible in part through funds received from an event that honors visionary achievements in automotive design.

"Vision Honored", the by-invitation-only pre-event black tie awards gala and dinner dance, was the inaugural benefit at Chrysler's new automotive design complex, Chrysler Technology Center (CTC) in Auburn Hills, Michigan. More than 500 members of the elite automotive design community gathered here to pay homage to Pininfarina and the late General Motors design legend, Harley Earl.

The complex, one of the largest known projects under construction in North America, measures 3.5 million square feet. Tons of granite, glass, steel and concrete form a spectacular structure. The Center's mission is just as hardlined and clear-cut: "To be the source of the best built, highest quality vehicles in the world while significantly reducing the cycle time from concept approval to volume production."

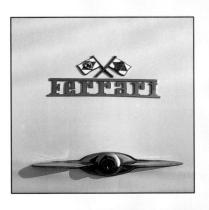

Mr. & Mrs. Sergio Pininfarina are surrounded by their children as a surprise wedding anniversary cake is presented during the gala.

Photo courtesy of GM Design

It was here, at Chrysler's magnificently designed new center, that Pininfarina and his lovely wife Giorgia were honored with an extraordinary cake in celebration of the couple's 40th wedding anniversary. Afterward, guests reviewed a video documentary of Pininfarina's body of work. At this time, Charles M. Jordan, vice president of design for General Motors and honorary "Eyes on the Classics" co-chairman, presented Pininfarina with a Steuben Crystal Arcus Award honoring his extraordinary 40-year association with Ferrari.

The choice of lead crystal glass to create the stunning Steuben Crystal Arcus Award is twofold: it shares similar properties with the human eye and it symbolizes the sophistication required of top-quality design. In scientific terms, crystal refracts light just like the human eye. In artistic terms, the name Steuben represents the best in crystal design. Furthermore, the differing refractive and dispersive qualities of lead crystal glass is what led to the development of the achromatic lens used in optical instruments to improve eyesight. Hence, it is the most appropriate form for the award to take.

The 1952 Ferrari 212 Inter-Cabriolet truly exemplifies the sleek lines and dramatic form of Pininfarina's art.

And what more appropriate place for the fourth annual "Eyes on the Classics" automotive show to take place but the classic grounds of the Edsel and Eleanor Ford House in Grosse Pointe Shores. Open to the public for just over six hours, more than 200 cars (an envious collection of rare an-

tiques, contemporary designs, and the latest concept vehicles) were on display during the event's "Private Eyes" brunch.

From the past, some of the most significant historical and antique vehicles were displayed; from the present, one current production vehicle from the three separate design teams of GM, Ford and Chrysler; and from the future, the latest concept vehicles from domestic automakers.

On the grounds of the Edsel and Eleanor Ford House: the 250 GT Lusso Berlinetta and, to its left, the original "buck" which Pininfarina used to mold the body of the car.

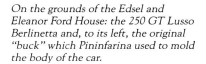

Sergio with his lovely wife Giorgia, sons Paolo (far left) and Andrea (far right) and daughter Lorenza.

The Pininfarina Display: from a Nash-Healey Roadster to an F-40 Berlinetta — examples of the diversity of Pininfarina's work.

A few of the highlights included: a **1900 Yale Touring; 1917 Miller Golden Submarine; 1917 Packard Model "E" Wingfoot Express; 1932 Cadillac Phaeton; 1936 Stout-Scarab Sedan; 1954 Mercedes-Benz 300 SL Gullwing Coupe; 1958 BMW 507 Roadster; and a 1959 Facel Vega Excellence Saloon.** Also featured were some of the finest automobiles designed by Sergio Pininfarina and Harley Earl, as well as an outstanding collection of 1950s "Motorama" cars.

The Ferrari 275 GTB/4 is majestic in appearance and further demonstrates Pininfarina's incredible flair for creating visual masterpieces.

Sergio takes a moment to autograph a copy of Rosso Ferrari/Three.

1991 "Eyes on the Classics" show were designed by nationally recognized illustrator and futurist designer, Syd Mead. Likewise, the 1990 "Eyes on the Classics" print was photographed by award-winning photographer Balthazar Korab. 🐎

"Eyes on the Classics" also has its eyes on tomorrow's designers. Scale models and drawings created by students from two of the top U.S. transportation design schools, Art Center College of Design, Los Angeles and Center for Creative Studies, Detroit, were also on display.

In keeping with the celebration of automotive design as art, commemorative posters of the

For information about the 1992 "Vision Honored" or sponsorship opportunities, contact the "Eyes on the Classics" Committee at (313) 824-5554 or write:

*Eyes on the Classics,
15415 East Jefferson Avenue,
Grosse Pointe Park, MI 48230.*

1991 Pininfarina Chronos prototype.

During the program, Sergio Pininfarina explained many of his design concepts to an enthusiastic crowd.
(Photo courtesy of GM Design)

OUTSTANDING CARS AND THEIR DESIGNERS HONORED AT

·1·9·9·1·

Eyes On The Classics

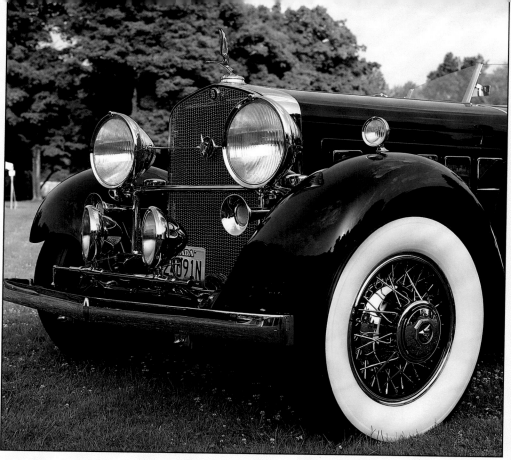

A classic in the truest sense of the word: the 1931 Pinin Farina-bodied V-16 Cadillac Convertible 4-Door, his first body design on an American chassis.

On June 30, 1991, more than 5,000 people came from all over the world to see the "Eyes on the Classics" automotive design show at the Edsel and Eleanor Ford House in Grosse Pointe Shores, Michigan.

The only show of its kind in the world, "Eyes on the Classics" honors outstanding automotive designers and celebrates past, present and future automotive design. Proceeds from the event support the Detroit Institute of Ophthalmology (DIO), a non-profit organization dedicated to helping the visually impaired through education and research.

General Motors President Lloyd Reuss served as honorary chairman for the 1991 event. Serving with him as honorary co-chairmen were the vice presidents of design for Chrysler, Ford and General Motors: Thomas C. Gale, John J. Telnack, Jr., and Charles M. Jordan, respectively. Richard Ruzzin, chief designer of General Motors' Cadillac Studio, served as the 1991 event chairman. Succeeding him for the 1992 "Eyes on the Classics" show is David Wenzler, vice president, Libbey-Owens-Ford.

Three vehicles in each of the 18 class categories were selected by a jury of automotive designers and honored with crystal awards for outstanding exterior and interior design. Also, three awards paid recognition to exceptional automobile design and were presented by the vice presidents of design for Chrysler, Ford and General Motors.

AWARDS AND WINNERS:

Photo courtesy of GM Design

Best in Show
Awarded by Judges
Steuben "Circle in the Square" Crystal Award
Winner: 1931 Studebaker President Four Seasons
        Roadster
Owner: S. Ray Miller, Jr., Elkhart IN

People's Choice
Steuben "Soaring Eagle"
Winner: 1952 Cisitalia Cabriolet
Owner: Scott Brayton, Coldwater, MI

Exhibitors' Choice
Awarded by Participants
Steuben "Soaring Eagle"
Winner: 1938 Chrysler Imperial Convertible Sedan
Owner: Diran Yazejian, Bloomfield Hills, MI

Automobile Design Example of Exceptional Merit
Steuben "Shooting Star" Crystal
Winner: 1948 Chrysler Town & Country Sedan
Owner: Len Deloia, Milford MI

Automobile Design Example of Exceptional Merit
Steuben "Shooting Star" Crystal
Winner: 1963 Ferrari 250 GT Lusso Berlinetta
Owner: Bob Larivee, Sr., Orion, MI

Automobile Design Example of Exceptional Merit
Steuben "Shooting Star" Crystal
Winner: 1931 Cadillac V-16 Body by Pininfarina
Owner: Robert Lee, Sparks NV

The Spirit of the Marque
Steuben "Trigon"
Winner: 1931 Chrysler Custom Imperial Lebaron
        Roadster
Owner: Lloyd Harriman, Troy MI

Best Example of Craftsmanship
(Original Design Execution)
Steuben "Star Crystal" Award
Winner: 1950 Ferrari Type 166 Berlinetta Stablimenti Farina
Owner: Glenn Hanke, Caledonia, WI

DESIGNERS' CHOICE AWARDS
Obelisk Crystal

Antiques — 1900 through 1925
Exterior Design Winner: 1925 Packard Roadster
Owner: William Howitt, Windsor, Ontario, Canada
Exterior Design Winner: 1910 Reo Touring
Owner: Rob Myers, Chatham, Ontario, Canada
Interior Design Winner: 1920 Milburn Electric
Owner: Jack Dunning, Cambridge, OH

American — 1926 through 1942
Exterior Design Winner: 1931 Studebaker President
                        Four Seasons Roadster
Owner: S. Ray Miller, Jr., Elkhart, IN
Exterior Design Winner: 1940 Lincoln Zephyr Club Coupe
Owner: W. Love, Sterling Heights, MI
Interior Design Winner: 1941 Cadillac Series 62 Convertible
Owner: Ed Meurer

European Post-War Luxury Convertible and Closed
Exterior Design Winner: 1948 Rolls Royce Silver
                        Wraith Hooper Saloon
Owner: Begnt Swenson, Franklin, MI

Exterior Design Winner: 1959 Facel Vega Excellence Saloon
Owner: Robert Carr, Ypsilanti, MI
Interior Design Winner: 1952 Mercedes 300S 2-Door Cabriolet
                        Convertible
Owner: Bernard Glieberman, W. Bloomfield, MI

American — 1946 through 1954
Exterior Design Winner: 1949 Buick Roadmaster Convertible
Owner: Marvin Tamaroff, Southfield
Exterior Design Winner: 1948 Packard Convertible
Owner: Don Sommer, Clawson, MI
Interior Design Winner: 1948 Ford Station Wagon
Owner: Keith Crain, Grosse Pointe, MI

American — 1955 through 1969
Exterior Design Winner: 1957 Ford Thunderbird 2-Door
Owner: David Rees, Farmington Hills, MI
Exterior Design Winner: 1957 Cadillac Eldorado Brougham
Owner: Dick Lannen, Birmingham, MI
Interior Design Winner: 1956 Chevrolet Bel Air Nomad
Owner: Ronald Wilson, Royal Oak, MI

European Pre-War (including Rolls Royces)
Exterior Design Winner: 1934 Riley Roadster
Owner: Robert Lutz, Ann Arbor, MI
Exterior Design Winner: 1938 Jaguar SS 100 Roadster
Owner: Mary Falvey, Fuller, Troy
Interior Design Winner: 1936 Mercedes-Benz 540 K
Owner: Marvin Tamaroff, Southfield

Post-War Classic Sports Car — 1946 through 1959
Exterior Design Winner: 1958 BMW 507
Owner: L. Jack Ruscilli, Columbus, OH
Exterior Design Winner: 1954 Jaguar XK-140 Roadster
Owner: James Yocum, Rochester Hills, MN
Interior Design Winner: 1954 Mercedes-Benz 300 SL
Gullwing Coupe
Owner: Jim Diamond, Grosse Isle, MI

Contemporary Sports Car — 1960 and Newer
Exterior Design Winner: 1965 Cobra 289 CSX2433
Owner: L. Jack Ruscilli, Columbus, OH
Exterior Design Winner: 1965 Griffith TVR 200 Coupe
Owner: James Whiting, Birmingham, MI
Interior Design Winner: 1965 Jaguar 4.2 E-Type Roadster
Owner: Bob Ackerman, W. Bloomfield

Honored Marque/Chrysler
Exterior Design Winner: 1955 Chrysler C-300 2-Door Hardtop
Owner: Buster Barone
Exterior Design Winner: 1941 Chrysler Town & Country
Owner: Peter Heydon, Ann Arbor, MI
Interior Design Winner: 1948 Chrysler Town & Country Sedan
Owner: Len Deloia, Milford MI

Honored Marque/Chrysler
Exterior Design Winner: 1931 Chrysler Custom Imperial
Dual Cowl Pheaton
Owner: William Chorkey, Farmington Hills, MI
Exterior Design Winner: 1960 Chrysler New Yorker 2-Door Hardtop
Owner: Vito Ranks, Harper Woods, MI

Unique Automotive Design Solution
Exterior Design Winner: 1962 Morris Mini Cooper MKL
Owner: Mark McChesney, Dearborn, MI
Exterior Design Winner: 1972 Citreon SM Coupe
Owner: David Rand, Birmingham, MI
Interior Design Winner: 1936 Stout-Scarab Sedan
Owner: Ronald Schneider, Franklin, MI

Racing Cars
Exterior Design Winner: 1917 Miller "Golden Submarine"
Owner: Robert "Buck" Boudeman, Richland, MI
Exterior Design Winner: 1965 Ford Mustang GT-350
Owner: Robert Varcoe, St. Clair Shores, MI
Interior Design Winner: 1970 Gurney AAR "CUDA"
Owner: Edward Skanes, Lexington, KY

American Muscle Cars
Exterior Design Winner: 1969 Ford Boss 429 Mustang
Owner: Keith Hishon, Romeo, MI
Exterior Design Winner: 1970 Dodge Challenger R/T 440 6-Pack
2-Door Hardtop
Owner: Robert Lees, Grosse Pointe, MI
Interior Design Winner: 1967 Shelby GT 500 Fastback
Owner: Brian Kaltz, Allen Park, MI

American Muscle Cars—"Friends of Vision" Award
Winner: 1970 Dodge Challenger R / T 440 6-Pack 2-Door Hardtop
Owner: Robert Lees, Grosse Pointe, MI

Commercial Vehicles
Exterior Design Winner: 1948 Hudson Pickup (prototype)
Owner: Charles Ruvolo, St. Clair Shores, MI
Exterior Design Winner: 1956 Chevrolet Cameo Carrier
Owner: Harold Reed, Whitmore Lake, MI
Interior Design Winner: 1959 Chevrolet El Camino Pickup
Owner: William Halsey, Mt. Clemens, MI

Sergio Pininfarina Design Awards (non-Ferrari)
Winner: 1959 Alfa Romeo Spyder Veloce
Owner: Hilary Raab, Jr., Crown Point, IN
Winner: 1967 Fiat Dino Spyder
Owner: Walter Sheldon, Jr., Lincolnshire, IL

Sergio Pininfarina Design Awards (Ferrari)
Winner: 1953 Ferrari 375 America Berlinetta
Owner: Hilary Raab, Jr., Crown Point, IN
Winner: 1963 Ferrari 250 GT Lusso Berlinetta
Owner: Bob Larivee, Sr., Orion, MI
Winner: 1972 Ferrari 365 GTB/4 Daytona Berlinetta
Owner: Don Kayko, Sr., Clarkston, MI
Winner: 1991 Ferrari F-40 Berlinetta
Owner: Chuck Jordan, Bloomfield Hills, MI

Harley Earl Design Awards
Exterior Design Winner: 1948 Buick Sedanette
Owner: Willard Smith, Grand Blanc, MI
Exterior Design Winner: 1959 Buick Electra 225 Convertible
Owner: Nicholas Chapekis, Ann Arbor, MI
Interior Design Winner: 1930 Cadillac V-16 Roadster
Owner: Richard Sahlin, Birmingham, MI

Photography by Brian King

Rosso Ferrari magazine commissioned renowned automotive writer, John Dinkel, Editor-at-Large of **Road & Track**, and internationally acclaimed automotive illustrator, Argentinian-born Hector Luis Bergandi, to present our readers with an exclusive portrait of Juan Manuel Fangio.

Both John and Hector spent time with Fangio to record his feelings about his past successes and his impressions about racing 34 years after his fifth, and last, World Championship. John's insights throughout the article are complemented by Hector's emotion-filled illustrations which capture the many moods of Juan Manuel Fangio throughout his remarkable racing career.

Fangio and Moss (right) were hailed equally as inspired talents of the racing world. At the Nurburgring in 1955, both were able to share the limelight.

...simply the greatest Grand Prix racing driver of all time.

Juan Manuel Fangio is quite simply the greatest Grand Prix racing driver of all time. Not only did he win a record five Grand Prix World Championships, but also his iron will, computer-like driving precision and his uncanny ability to take calculated risks that always paid off combined to produce a dominant driving force during the 1950s that was both feared and admired by his contemporaries.

Mercedes-Benz photo

On June 24, 1991 Juan Manuel Fangio celebrated his 80th birthday. In honor of that occasion, Pirelli sponsored a book called ***Fangio-A Pirelli Album*** by Stirling Moss with Doug Nye in association with Mercedes-Benz. The book was unveiled to the world's automotive press in late April in Stuttgart, Germany, home of Mercedes-Benz. Part of the two days of activities included ceremonial laps around the Hockenheim circuit by Fangio and Moss in a W 196 and a 300SLR which Mercedes had plucked from its marvelous museum. These cars dominated Grand Prix and sports car racing during the mid-Fifties.

There is no one better suited to write a book on Fangio than Stirling Moss, Fangio's one-time rival, teammate and close friend. Moss, winner of 16 Grand Prix and four time runner-up in the World Drivers' Championship, competed against Fangio for much of his F1 racing career, and the two men formed the all-conquering Mercedes-Benz team of 1955.

Moss, who probably followed Fangio for more racing miles than any other driver, unabashedly calls Fangio the greatest driver of them all. The driver who could always go that little bit quicker, for that little bit longer. The driver who demonstrated how fast one should go and just how clean driving should be. The man who understood the responsibility of being champion. A man who appreciated his mechanics and his cars. A man whose word was a contract. A man who always remembered those who had helped him.

Mercedes-Benz returned to Grand Prix racing at the French Grand Prix at Reims on July 4, 1954. Fangio took pole position in his W 196 streamliner (18) from teammates Karl Kling and Alberto Ascari in the Lancia Ferrari. Fangio won.
(Mercedes-Benz photo)

Fangio was born in Argentina of immigrant Italian parents in the small town of Balcarce, which is located about 190 miles south of Buenos Aires and an hour's drive away from Mar del Plata. He became involved with automobiles when he was about 11, spending afternoons at a local garage and developing the "feel" for machinery that helped him throughout his racing career. By the time he was 16, young Juan Manuel was maturing, not only as a skilled mechanic but also as a driver. The owner of the Studebaker dealership he worked for made Juan drive as soon as he started there, in all sorts of weather, over long distances and through difficult terrain, much of it unpaved roads.

Juan Manuel Fangio with the famous Balcarce Chevrolet with which he dominated road racing in the 1940s. This picture was taken on the outskirts of Balcarce, where Fangio still makes his home.
(Road & Track photo)

Fangio won the Italian Grand Prix in 1954 and 1955 behind the wheel of the Mercedes W 196.
(Mercedes-Benz photo)

"I felt I was a good driver, even at this age," remembers Fangio.

His first race cars were essentially road cars with their bodies and fenders removed. Fangio competed in circle track as well as road races, developing a reputation in the latter, which in those days were mainly cross-country endurance events similar to Mexico's Carrera Pan Americana, not close-circuit road courses as we are most familiar with today. In 1939, Fangio entered the Grand Prix of Argentina, one of those mostly off-road enduros, in a Chevy coupe that was a gift from his friends and fans in Balcarce. He started 108th and finished 5th. The following year he won the race as a member of the Chevrolet factory team.

Fangio's first European appearance was at Reims in 1948 in a Simca Gordini which failed to fin-

ish. He was 37 years old at the time, an age when many racing drivers would have been thinking about retiring. Stirling Moss recounts the fact that it was at Reims in July of 1949 that he first drove in a race with Fangio. He was 19, half Fangio's age! Fangio started from pole position in a Ferrari Tipo 166 F2, the same model he had driven for the first time one month before in winning the Grand Prix of Monza. In the charmingly-named Coupe des Petites Cylindrees at Reims, Fangio set fastest lap before his gearbox packed up. Moss also retired, victim of a drive-chain failure in his air-cooled rear-engine Cooper.

From being a virtual unknown in Europe in 1948, Fangio burst spectacularly upon the scene the following year in a Maserati 4CLT/48 sponsored by the Automobile Club of Argentina. He won six European Grand Prix races, including his aforementioned victory at Monza in a Ferrari Tipo 166 F2.

In 1950, Fangio counted seven Grand Prix victories among his many wins, and he placed second in the inaugural World Drivers' Championship to his Alfa teammate Giuseppe Farina. Fangio finished the season with three races in South America, winning two in a Ferrari Tipo 166C and the third in a Talbot-Lago.

Fangio was back with Alfa for the 1951 season, the Tipo 158 having given way to the Tipo 159. Starting in late May he won four of the last eight Grand Prix run that year and placed second in two others, garnering enough points to win the World Championship.

The 1952 racing season started off in dramatic fashion with Fangio winning six of seven South American races in a Ferrari Tipo 166C. Back in Europe for the Grand Prix of Monza, Fangio suffered the only major injury of his entire career. On the second lap of the race he lost control of his Maserati A6GCM which skidded off the track and launched itself, ejecting Fangio from the cockpit.

Monza, 1956 — Italian Grand Prix. Fangio and Castellotti at the right rear of the car during practice. Also pictured at the rear of the racing car is Manicardi, the team mechanic. Note the spectators overhead on the pit balcony, a favored spot for photographers in the old days.

He landed in the grass, breaking a vertebra in a fall that left him unconscious for several hours and put him out of racing for the rest of the season.

Fangio blames the accident on fatigue. He had started out from Ireland the previous afternoon expecting a relaxed airplane ride to take him to Monza. Unfortunately, bad weather had grounded all flights from Paris, and Fangio had driven all night and reached Monza only a half hour before the

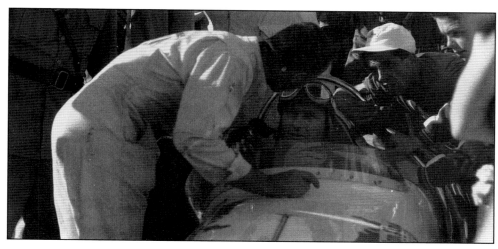

Monza, 1958. Fangio tries out the cockpit of the Dean Van Lines Special from Indianapolis. Piero Taruffi is second from left. Fangio was fourth fastest qualifier, but did not start due to engine problems.
(Photos by Jesse Alexander)

start of the race. A lesser man would have stopped and rested... and missed the race. Not Fangio. He had given his word to Omer Orsi of Maserati that he would drive the A6GCM when it made its debut, and to Fangio his word was more binding than any piece of paper.

The scene is the finish line at Ciudad Juarez, Mexico after the 1953 Carrera Pan Americana. Fangio crosses the line with his riding mechanic in the Lancia D24 sports car having won the race at an average speed of 169.2 kph.

Fangio returned to racing in 1953, achieving moderate success with the Maserati, winning two Grand Prix and placing second in five others. Alberto Ascari won the World Drivers' Championship in a Ferrari 500 F2, repeating his championship of the previous year.

From 1954 through 1957 Fangio dominated Grand Prix racing like no other before or since. He was World Champion four years running, twice in a Mercedes W196, once in a Lancia Ferrari V-8 and the last time in an outclassed Maserati 250F that Fangio literally willed to victory.

Juan Manuel Fangio retired from racing in 1958. He was 47 and had considered retiring even before the clutch pedal of his Maserati had broken off 24 laps

into the French Grand Prix at Reims. *"Racing no longer gave me satisfaction; it had become an obligation. And when racing begins to feel like work, well..."*

Today, Juan Manuel Fangio is honorary president of the Automobile Club of Argentina, as well as President of Mercedes-Benz Argentina S.A. A Mercedes agency in Mar del Plata also bears his name. But his life's work, his own museum, has been established at home in the Town Hall of Balcarce. In close cooperation with the Mercedes Museum in Unterturkheim, a permanent automobile and historic exhibition has been put together, initiated and

run by the Juan Manuel Fangio Foundation. His dream is that the house where he grew up and where he still lives today will one day become part of the museum, too.

My time with Fangio for this story was short but sweet. In fact, this interview might never have happened except that fate, Lady Luck and two good friends from Pirelli, Bob Newman and Geno Effler, interceded on my behalf. I was one among literally hundreds of journalists who had been invited to Fangio's birthday celebration, each hoping for even a moment alone with the Maestro.

My few minutes, arranged by Effler, were to come during the ride back from the birthday dinner at the Mercedes museum to Fangio's hotel. It had been a long day for Juan. In truth, it had been a long week of virtually non-stop activities. As Fangio got into the rear of the Mercedes it was well

Fangio in the pits at Monza in 1956.
(Photos by Jesse Alexander)

ONCE AGAIN, PIRELLI MAKES A GENEROUS CONTRIBUTION
TO THE PERFORMING ARTS.

Original equipment tires on the world's finest.

The 1956 12 Hours of Sebring.

*F*angio driving the Ferrari 860 Monza to victory in the 12 Hours of Sebring. The Ferrari team of Fangio-Castellotti presented a major challenge to the competition. The 860 was one of Fangio's favorite cars. He felt that the 860 was "awesome" and was one of the most powerful "big" Ferrari race cars ever built. His victory at Sebring was Juan's first racing victory in the United States.

Juan Manuel Fangio...

The 1956 British Grand Prix at Silverstone.

The race was fought between Mike Hawthorn in the newest BRM, Stirling Moss with the Maserati 250 F, Tony Brooks with a short wheelbase BRM, and Fangio in the Ferrari D50.

Early in the race, Fangio spun out in Beckett's turn dueling with Hawthorn, but regained his position as the race progressed.

Tony Brooks developed a major throttle problem, making the BRM very difficult to drive. In the Abbey turn, Brooks lost control and overturned the car. He was thrown out of the car, clear of the fire with only his pride hurting.

Fangio drove a very deliberate, calculating race, pacing himself in order to advance his position.

Hawthorn developed mechanical problems and retired from the race. Moss also had problems and pitted, enabling Fangio to take the lead for good.

It was one of Juan's many great races and his first victory in England.

past midnight, and I could tell he was tired. Who wouldn't be? Unfortunately, in the confusion of the moment, his translator (Fangio speaks fluent Spanish and Italian, but little English) wound up in another car and I was left having to ask my questions in English to Fangio's female companion, a lovely woman with a good command of English, but who had difficulty hearing my questions and correctly interpreting Fangio's answers in the somewhat noisy car.

I wanted to know what Fangio considered his best race in a Ferrari. The answer was, *"Many great racers have driven Ferraris."* It was one of those instances when nothing was going right, and there was nothing I could do to right the situation. Mercifully, for all concerned, the ride was soon over. Fangio exited the car and was whisked away into the hotel.

Awkwardly, I tried to thank Fangio's companion for her help in interpreting my questions. She, in turn, apologized profusely for her lack of English and for Juan's lack of enthusiasm, explaining that he had been in enormous discomfort the entire day because of neck

pain, a lasting reminder of his crash at Monza in 1952. Twice that day Fangio had received injections to numb the pain, and these injections had not only contributed to his sleepiness, but also to an upset stomach.

I walked into the hotel lobby and was met by Effler, who was to drive me back to my hotel. We walked to the parking garage and spent the next 15 minutes hunting for the car. By now it was close to

one in the morning, and I was one tired and depressed journalist. My once-in-a-lifetime opportunity to interview the great Juan Manuel Fangio had just slipped through my fingers—and my tongue. I thought back to my three years of high school Spanish, wishing I had been more diligent with the conversational portions of my lessons. What do they say, hindsight is always veinte-veinte?

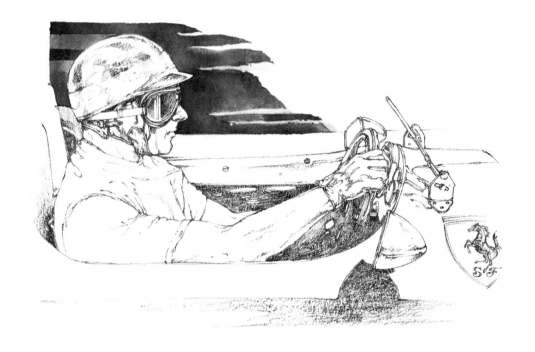

Juan Manuel Fangio in the cockpit of the D50.

And, adding insult to injury, I might have to walk the three miles back to my hotel! We checked both parking levels twice, finally realizing that the level closest to the street could only be reached from the hotel lobby. We trudged up a flight of stairs and were walking through the lobby when a female voice with a familiar Spanish accent cried out, *"John, John."* Geno and I both turned around to see Juan Manuel Fangio and his lady friend sitting on a couch in the lobby. She waved us over and said, *"Please, you must sit down. Juan feels very badly that he could not give you a good interview in the car. It has been a long day for Juan and he is very tired. But he remembers all the journalists who helped him during his career. And he could not sleep knowing that he had not done his best for you."*

At that very moment, Bob Newman, who is head of Pirelli's European public relations efforts and who conceived the idea of ***Fangio-A Pirelli Album***, happened to walk through the lobby. Spying the four of us huddled in a corner, he wandered on over. Bob speaks fluent Italian, and, through his assistance, I was able to pose many of my questions.

Monaco, 1956. Fangio during Grand Prix practice.
(Photo by Jesse Alexander)

A picture which hangs in the Fangio Museum in his Argentine hometown of Balcarce vividly displays the characteristic Fangio racing pose.
(Mercedes-Benz photo)

The next happenstance that made this story possible was a phone call to Hector Luis Bergandi, the enormously talented Argentine illustrator and writer who is Juan Manuel Fangio's personal friend. I queried Bergandi as to whether he could envision some illustrations to accompany this interview. Not only would he create some original artwork, but Bergandi also volunteered to call Fangio in Argentina to fill in a few gaps in my interview.

That one simple phone call evolved into several calls and lots of sleuthing on Bergandi's part to track Fangio down. He wasn't in Argentina. Rather he was on holiday in Santo Domingo, and according to Bergandi, the phone connection was like being in an echo chamber

The start of the tragic 1955 24 Hour race at Le Mans. Fangio had difficulty getting his 300SLR started and can be seen up against the pit wall with two mechanics working on the car. It was the 300SLR of Fangio's teammate Pierre Levegh (20) and the Austin-Healey (26) of Lance Macklin that were involved in the terrible accident.

and hearing yourself talking with a four second delay. As a result, Hector was unable to pose all the questions he had hoped to ask. Later, I sat down with Hector, and we primarily chatted about 1956, that pivotal year in Fangio's career when he raced as part of the Ferrari factory team. Our discussions included previous conversations Bergandi had had with Fangio, as well as his most recent phone call. As a result, I have broken that portion of this article into a separate extended sidebar in which Fangio's and Bergandi's thoughts could be expressed, separate from the purely question-and-answer portions of my interview.

This story wouldn't have been possible without the commitment of ***Rosso Ferrari*** and without the assistance I received from Pirelli, Mercedes-Benz, Hector Luis Bergandi and, most of all, from Juan Manuel Fangio. The result is a unique insight into the greatest racing driver of all time, Juan Manuel Fangio, truly a man among men and a gentleman among gentlemen.

What do you remember about your first race?

It went from Buenos Aires to Lima to Buenos Aires. We were on the road for weeks. There were only very few asphalted road surfaces.

Who were your toughest competitors?

Without hesitation, I would say they were Stirling Moss and Alberto Ascari. Both were highly gifted racing drivers.

How did you view your own talent?

During a race, I thought all the time that I was the best.

Contemporaries like to say you were simpatico with your race cars and your mechanics.

I always talked to my cars. I can hear when a car is not feeling its best. It is like music when an instrument is playing out of tune. I always spoke Italian to the Mercedes mechanics. I think the results show that they must have all understood me.

What was your favorite race track?

There is no doubt it is the Northern Loop of the Nurburgring, an extremely old track. You

Fangio and racing cars are still inseparable. When he got together with the W 196 again in 1991, Fangio said, "It feels as though I am meeting a favorite child again."

can only drive it fast if you know it like the back of your hand.

Tell me about racing manners and sportsmanship, today and when you were racing.

The problem always boils down to money, to the obligations to sponsors. In our day, drivers who did not know the rules of sportsmanship on the track were simply ignored by the others at the evening gala dinners. Nowadays, this type of organized event does not happen. No one has the time to spare any more. But there has always been bad behavior on the race track, and there always will be.

Is it possible to compare race drivers today and when you raced?

To say that Senna drives like Fangio, or Prost like Moss or vice versa is simply absurd.

What about friendships among drivers?

It would be a good thing if friendships developed. But on the racing track we were all enemies.

More than 30 years after you retired from racing, you are still probably the best known personality from Argentina. Can you describe how that makes you feel?

I do not consider the honor done to me by my compatriots and others to be a burden, but praise for a job well done. And I am grateful for it. I still have all my trophies. They are not mine; instead, they belong to all those who have supported me.

Speaking of support, your partnership with Pirelli spanned your entire Grand Prix career. Tell me how you became associated with Pirelli.

Pirelli helped me when no one knew Fangio. When I first came to Europe with my Equipo Argentino, we had very little money. Pirelli gave me tires on a "race now, pay later" basis. These are things one never forgets.

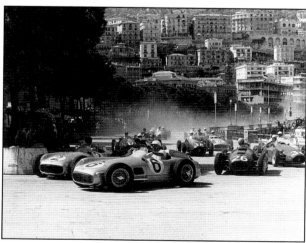

Fangio (2) with his two greatest rivals, Moss (6) and Alberto Ascari (Lancia Ferrari - 26) at the start of the 1955 Monaco Grand Prix.

Grand Prix d'Europe, Monte Carlo, May 22, 1955. Juan behind the wheel of his latest-model short-wheelbase Mercedes-Benz W 196 with outboard front brakes. Fangio much preferred this version to the older long-wheelbase inboard front-brake design.

(Mercedes-Benz photos)

Do you regret not racing at the Indianapolis 500?

Yes, but I had a car that was no good. I am sorry I didn't race, but I knew I could do nothing with that car. I asked myself, "What is the World Champion doing, trying to win with a car that he knows doesn't have a chance?" The car was three years old and the mechanics knew nothing about it. The mechanics didn't even know how to make simple adjustments to the car. In fact, they didn't even know the name of a spare part we needed. I had to explain to another mechanic. They got the part and couldn't install it. I couldn't speak English, but at least I knew how to do that.

I felt I had a responsibility to my title as World Champion and to all the other people I represented. It would have reflected poorly on everyone racing in Europe to have a World Champion come to America and not perform well.

But I have fond memories of the time I spent at Indy. I was very surprised how the top drivers accepted me. I was a foreigner...a newcomer. I didn't speak English. I expected them to view me as an outsider who was coming from road racing to perhaps steal their race. Instead they received me with open arms and good will. These men were stars, yet they went out of their way to help me in every way.

What did you take from other parts of your life that helped you become a World Champion?

You do it with experience and time. You don't go to Formula One right away. I did my training in Argentina. I won the Lima-Buenos Aires 10,000 kilometer. That kind of race experience contributed to my Grand Prix successes. I was also a mechanic, which helped me enormously throughout my career. The driver carries the name, but it's the mechanics who make you win. This is probably a major ingredient in my victories, my successes. I always considered the needs of the mechanics, and I got along extremely well with them because, apart from anything else, I was a mechanic. As a result, human beings being what they are, they did their very best for me. Perhaps their best was a greater best than what they did for other people.

What do you remember most about your first race in Europe?

I went to France in 1948 as a spectator at the French Grand Prix at Reims. And Amedee Gordini, who had seen me race a Simca-Gordini at Rosario, asked, "Would you like to drive a Gordini?" And I was a spectator. That was the very first race of my career in Europe. Years later I went back to race for Gordini, and I did so when I was World Champion for nothing, because he let me race in 1948 for nothing.

Mille Miglia, 1956. Fangio with Castellotti.
(Photo by Jesse Alexander)

August 17, 1991.
Hector Luis Bergandi and Juan Manuel Fangio at
the Monterey Historic Automobile Races.
(Photo by Brian King)

Reflections on 1956, Fangio's year with Ferrari, from information gathered from conversations between Juan Manuel Fangio and Hector Luis Bergandi.

1956 was a point in Formula 1 history when a lot of things happened to produce a World Championship for Ferrari. Alberto Ascari dominated the Championship in 1952 and 1953 driving the Ferrari F2 car, but the following two years Ferrari was rather uncompetitive, compared with Mercedes-Benz, for example. Lampredi, the designer of the F2, had on paper a design for a new engine and a new car, but Ferrari was in debt and his small operation was on the verge of bankruptcy. Fangio had gone to Europe with the hope of winning one more championship and had already won his third and might be giving some thought to retiring and going back to Argentina to take care of his Mercedes-Benz dealership. Meanwhile, Lancia had had success with the D50, not against the all-conquering Mercedes-Benz W196, but at least the organization was moving in the right direction.

All of a sudden things happened in a way that changed all the protagonists. The catalyst was the accident at Le Mans in 1955. That accident was a catastrophe. It caused many people to view racing as immoral because of the danger it posed, not only to the drivers, but to the spectators. That accident, along with Ascari's death at Monza, prompted Lancia to consider quitting racing. Ascari had been such an important driver. So much of the weight of the Lancia program had been placed on his shoulders. Suddenly, auto racing in Italy was in total jeopardy. This is when the president of the Automobile Club of Italy came forth with the idea of using Fiat funds, the cars from the Lancia and Ferrari organization to create an Italian racing team that would save the D50s from being sold for scrap and Ferrari from bankruptcy. And Fangio was available because Mercedes had retired from racing.

Fangio and Ferrari had a first meeting where Ferrari said, *"I need you very much,"* but things weren't resolved and became somewhat complicated. Fangio noticed that

racing was changing, and when he finally agreed to race for Ferrari, he opted for an agent to take care of the financial arrangements and the terms of the contract. At the same time, Fangio was having problems in Argentina, because the Peron government had been taken down by a revolution and nobody was above suspicion. Peron had been supportive of all forms of sport, and because Juan was such a successful sportsman, some within the revolutionary government thought Fangio might

Monaco, 1956. Practice for the Grand Prix, and Fangio tries out the Lancia Ferrari cockpit. Note the early morning light. Practice at Monaco was often held before breakfast.
(Photo by Jesse Alexander)

Fangio at the wheel of the beautifully restored Maserati 250F in which he won his greatest race, the 1957 German Grand Prix at the Nurburgring. This photo was taken in June 1990 at the Nurburgring, site of that 1957 race, during which Fangio won his fifth World Drivers' Championship.
(Road & Track photo)

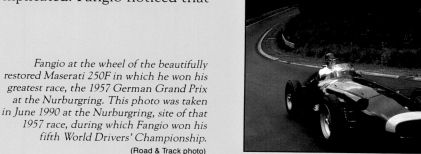

have taken advantage of his position. It turned out that the investigator who was making life miserable for Juan was actually a crook. Finally Juan went to the authorities and said, *"Do what you have to do, but do it now and let me know if I will be able to continue in business and to leave the country to race."* All suspicions about Juan were put aside, and going back to Europe to race was a great relief.

Juan liked the Lancia D50 very much. The car was very low to the ground and very stable. During the winter, Ferrari had moved the fuel tank to the rear of the car—it was originally in the side pods—and had sealed the gap between the bodywork and the side pods so that the D50 was a more integrated design with better aerodynamics. Juan recalls that it was actually a very nice car to drive, although it was a car that had teeth. It had shown that side of its personality when it threw Ascari into the sea at Monaco in 1955. Only drivers with the skill of an Ascari or a Fangio could actually go fast in those cars. Driven a notch below their limits, they were fine. Pushed to the limit, they could bite you. It was common in 1956 for the drivers to spin the car. Fortunately, there were no serious accidents.

People who watched the Monaco race that year remember Fangio doing strange things, hitting walls, for example, and the car was actually very bent despite the fact that the Maestro was driving it. Those who witnessed that race remember him as being enraged, which was uncharacteristic of Fangio. He was always so relaxed, driving with the finger tips. But that time he was really angry at his car.

A series of events had happened that upset Fangio with the way things were going with Ferrari. For example, at the Mille Miglia in April he had a problem with water filling the cockpit of his 290 MM. He stopped and asked the mechanics to cut holes to allow the water to drain, because his feet

Fangio driving the Ferrari 290 MM in the 1956 Mille Miglia. The 600 number designation was Fangio's starting time: 6:00 a.m.

were freezing. But all he got was another hole that started spraying water up on his body. He couldn't get his hands off the steering wheel, because his fingers were frozen in a clenched position. Worse, water was spraying under his visor, and his face looked like he had been beaten by a boxer. A normal person could not have taken the pain. Coming into Modena he stopped at a restaurant where he was a regular customer, and someone was kind enough to give him a leather jacket and a glass of cognac which he drank just to get his blood circulating. Somehow Fangio managed to finish the race in 4th place, but for a long time there was nothing that would ease the pain.

Then came Monaco, where he finished 2nd with the car of Peter Collins, followed by a series of retirements and 2nd- and 3rd-place finishes leading up to the French Grand Prix at Reims in July. Here he was doing well when

suddenly he began to feel cold and wet. Fuel was leaking from the pressure gauge. Fangio says it was one of the few times he was concerned about his safety, because either a spark or a backfire from the exhaust would have roasted him. At the time of the leak, he felt he was in a position to win the race. Lesser men would have quit, but Juan nursed the car to a 4th-place finish.

Because of incidents such as these, Juan began to feel uncomfortable with the Ferrari team management. When Bergandi asked Fangio what his best race was with the Lancia Ferrari, he replied, *"Obviously the German Grand Prix at the Nurburgring. There I excelled and performed the way a champion should."*

But when Bergandi said, *"I am going to do a painting of you at the Silverstone Grand Prix for this article,"* Fangio thought for a few moments and then said, *"Well, yes, that is actually a valuable race*

Mauro Povia leans against a Pirelli Stelvio tire, fitted to an Alfa Romeo 159, the car that took Fangio to his first World Championship in 1951. Povia, now 70, was one of Pirelli's two Grand Prix tire fitters from 1950 until 1958, and he made a significant contribution to Fangio's victory in the 1957 German Grand Prix.
(Road & Track photo)

in my memory because it took place just two weeks after Reims, and I had such severe chemical burns that when I went through my pre-race physical the doctor said, 'You cannot race. You are too badly burned.' To that I smiled and said, 'If you want to tell the organizers that I am not going to run, that is okay with me. That's up to you.' And when the doctor went to the organizers he said, 'He runs!'"

Fangio was the reigning World Champion, and he wanted to race if he could. In fact, he won the race with an incredibly inspired performance, but he was in severe pain the entire time because of his burns.

Fangio at Spa in 1956 in the Lancia Ferrari, cornering at the La Source hairpin. Note the changes to the body work since Monaco.
(Photo by Jesse Alexander)

At mid-year, Ferrari was in good shape to fight for the championship, although there was a feeling of uneasiness surrounding the team. After the French Grand Prix, Fangio said to Enzo Ferrari, *"I went to the Mille Miglia and you got me frozen. Then I went to France, and you almost got me roasted. I want a mechanic who is going to take good care of only my car or I would rather leave the team right now."*

Enzo Ferrari replied, *"No, no. We don't want you to stop. We are going to provide you with a mechanic you feel comfortable with."*

After that meeting, things changed dramatically. Fangio immediately won at Silverstone and then at the Nurburgring, in what was actually his best race of the year. Juan displayed his true World Champion form, winning the race with style and dominance.

The showdown for the 1956 World Championship occurred at Monza in the Italian GP, the last race of the year counting toward the Championship. During the race, Fangio's Lancia Ferrari suffered a broken steering arm, which put his car out of the race. Juan spent 19 laps in the pits while his teammate Luigi Musso ignored signals to pull in and hand his car over to the World Champion. He still refused when he came in to change tires.

"How did you feel at the time?" Bergandi asked.

"I felt very disappointed," Fangio replied. *"I could see the World Championship slipping away."*

Then Bergandi asked, *"How did you feel when Musso refused to give you his car?"*

"I accepted it," Fangio replied. *"I wasn't upset by his attitude, because I could understand what it was like for a young driver to feel*

Fangio in the Lancia Ferrari D50 at Monaco in 1956. The "p" indicates "practice" as Fangio was trying out the car for the first time.
(Photo by Jesse Alexander)

This picture was taken at Silverstone in the mid-Fifties. Fangio and Peter Collins are both on the Ferrari team. Notice the goggles and the light weight Herbert Johnson polo helmet.
(Photo by Jesse Alexander)

that he had a chance to win his home Grand Prix. He was so intense about continuing to race and defending his chance to win that he just refused to give his car to his team leader. Then Peter Collins came in to change his rear tires, saw me standing outside my car and offered me his car without being asked."

That [Bergandi speaking] I would say is the mark of someone who probably had a high level of confidence in himself. Collins was a mature young man. He probably felt that if he won the World Championship because Fangio's car had broken, it would have been like stealing. Collins had won only 2-3 races before being placed in that situation, and he probably thought, "It's too early for me. I

would rather be a good teammate and give the World Champion the chance to defend what is his." And perhaps he was so much of a sportsman that today we are not prepared to accept that anyone could be so devoid of selfishness.

Fangio took over Collins car and finished 2nd to Stirling Moss, but the points he scored were enough to make him World Champion for a fourth time.

Bergandi asked about the respect shown for Fangio by other drivers, to which Juan replied, "It's true that they showed me respect in many ways. One of the most fantastic was the way the Ferrari drivers treated me when I beat them with the Maserati at the

Nurburgring in 1957 [By all accounts, Fangio's greatest race—Ed.]. They were so happy for me it was like they were my fans, not my competitors."

The other drivers respected Fangio, because they thought of him as a teacher.

"As you know," Bergandi continued, "the actual meaning of the word 'maestro' is teacher, not a unique performer. Other drivers followed Fangio to find out how he did things. He was someone from whom they learned everything they knew. Even so, they couldn't catch up to him. The other drivers acknowledged that his was a unique talent."

Fangio in the Ferrari D50 at the 1956 German Grand Prix.
The D50 was modified with changes in the suspension system and was more streamlined with an elongated nose. The changes made the D50 extremely fast and very easy to drive. For Fangio the car was "fun" to drive...fun because he was Fangio. Notice the blue and yellow international racing colors of Argentina that were painted on the nose of the D50 for this particular race.

"I love Ferrari cars more than I love my wife."
Giancarlo Donnini

the MODENA GARAGEMAN

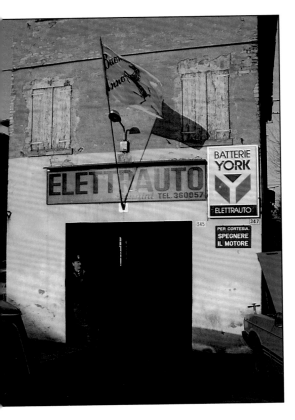

It's so small, you might pass it without noticing: a small one-car shop on a main road in Modena. From the outside, it is a very ordinary non-descript repair shop — set back from the busy street. Drive by on your way to the Fini Hotel, the unofficial hotel of Ferrari, and the one thing you might notice about this small town shop is a flag hanging outside. Bright yellow, with a familiar black prancing horse. It seems so out of place, it piques your interest. Pass by when the bay door is up, and what you see may floor you. Wall-to-wall Ferrari memorabilia. Posters autographed in signature purple by Enzo Ferrari himself. Yards of press clippings tacked carefully to the walls. Miles of candid photographs of Mr. Ferrari. All of it captures the heart and soul of the Ferrari mystique, especially since Enzo Ferrari himself had been there. He had to see with his own eyes what everyone else in town talked about: Giancarlo Donnini's living tribute to Enzo Ferrari. What man could resist paying a visit to one of his most enthusiastic fans?

Fifty-two year old Giancarlo Donnini has witnessed much of Ferrari's history first-hand, all from his small quiet shop. *Rosso Ferrari* was able to capture some of Mr. Donnini's memories, thanks to the help of Filomena Marino, from a nearby dress shop

who was able to interpret for us. With warm affection, Mr. Donnini recalled his visits by Mr. Ferrari as accurately as any loyal fan would record events of such historic proportions. "*Mr. Ferrari visited me three times . . . each time he brought a poster that he put his signature on. This made me feel honored. That a man who has done so much for Modena . . . Italy . . . and the world . . . that he would come visit a neighborhood mechanic.*"

Everyday for the last thirty years, Giancarlo Donnini has looked outside beyond his shop to catch a glimpse of a Ferrari racing by. He worships the road a Ferrari drives on. This is not unusual. But it is ironic, considering that Mr. Donnini has never had the opportunity to do any work on a Ferrari. Still, the allure that Mr. Ferrari's handiwork holds for Mr. Donnini is as powerful as a two-ton magnet.

"*I love Ferrari cars more than I love my wife*," gushed Mr. Donnini. *The ultimate fan.* What else could you call a man who would admit that publicly — and live to tell about it? Added Mr. Donnini, "*I attended every Ferrari function, even if I was sick!*" That's just the sort of loyalty and devotion that Enzo Ferrari was capable of inspir-

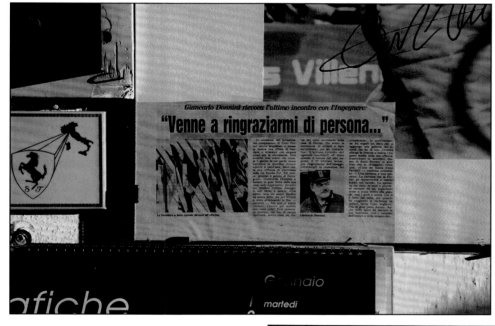

Mr. Donnini's love for Ferrari can be seen in his eyes as well as on the walls of his shop.

*Mr. Donnini is very proud
of his posters signed
by Mr. Ferrari.*

ing in people, whether they were the engineers and designers who worked for him or local people like Giancarlo Donnini. This is why the mortal man, Enzo Ferrari, lives on in people's hearts, while the legendary Ferrari lives on in the annals of automotive history.

So, if you ever happen to be in Modena on your way to the Fini Hotel, slow down and look for a bright yellow flag with the black prancing horse hanging outside a small automotive repair shop that doesn't look like much from the outside. Stop by and say hello to Giancarlo Donnini. Ask what he thinks the key to Ferrari's success was and he'll tell you, "*His determination. That made all the difference.*" And just maybe, the support and devotion of nice people like Giancarlo Donnini had something to do with it as well.

*Story and Photography by Hank Forssberg
and Nancy Talarico*

*Say hello to Mr. Donnini
from all of us at
Rosso Ferrari on your next
trip to Modena.*

the PHARMACIST

Mr. Ferrari's autographed picture and other mementos are proudly displayed in the pharmacy.

Imagine for a moment that you are once again a young boy. You are in Maranello, Italy — that's where you were born. Your father is the local pharmacist — there aren't many around. Someone very special is coming to dinner tonight. Your mother warns you, "Be careful, there's a very important man coming to dinner: Mr. Ferrari."

This is an experience you will never forget.

For 40 years, Gastone Caselli was Enzo Ferrari's pharmacist. They were two locals, two professional businessmen. Over the years, they shared countless conversations over many dinners. Some of these conversations have been committed to memory by the young boy who dutifully obeyed his mother's forewarning — Riccardo, Gastone's son.

"The first time I was allowed to have dinner at home when Mr. Ferrari came, my mother told me, 'Be careful, there's a very important man coming to dinner: Mr. Ferrari.' Because of that, I behaved," recalled Riccardo.

"It was such an important occasion that my father bought me my first tie. So, we are all sitting around the table, soup has been served, and I notice Mr. Ferrari looking at me. I looked down, and there was my brand new tie resting in the soup! Fortunately for me, Mr. Ferrari just laughed."

"On another occasion, my father brought me to one of these dinners with Mr. Ferrari and his drivers. I remember overhearing that one of the drivers had had an accident, and I heard people saying that he had screws and bolts put into his leg. So, I wanted to see this for myself, a man with screws and bolts sticking out of his leg. So, I wandered over to the driver and very nicely touched his leg to see if there really were screws sticking out!"

"I have another vivid memory of a conversation between my father and Mr. Ferrari. It went something like this: *'I have signed this new driver,'* said Ferrari. *'He's good. I like him very much. But this boy breaks cars at such a high rate, and cars are expensive. I don't know what to do.'* My father said, 'Okay, but think about this. What if he goes to another racing team and becomes a very good driver? Think about the consequences.' And so Ferrari said, *'You are right. I'll keep him!'*"

And so, the legend continues, generation after generation. Although Enzo Ferrari and Gastone are no longer able to sit across the table from each other and talk shop, the impact Mr. Ferrari had on one man's young son lives on in Riccardo's heart as well as his memory. Evidence of this devotion is visible to this day. Inside the pharmacy, arranged as one would display family photos, a big old chest comfortably sits, boasting photo after photo of Enzo Ferrari, as well as original correspondence . . .each a cherished souvenir belonging to a boy at heart — a boy who will look up to his hero today, tomorrow, and always. 🐎

Riccardo Caselli and Gianni Rogliatti.

Story and Photography by Hank Forssberg and Nancy Talarico

Protect Your Most Valuable Investment

Keep Your Car in Mint Condition with Genuine Ferrari Parts and Service

Your Ferrari deserves the level of care that only a factory-authorized Ferrari dealer can provide.

Factory-trained technicians understand the advanced engineering of your car and maintain its performance with Ferrari race-tested parts.

Take no chances. Rely on "the best" for "the best".

Genuine Ferrari parts and service... an investment in your car's future.

Genuine Ferrari Parts and Service Are Available Only Through Your Authorized Ferrari Dealer

GENUINE

Ferrari ®

PARTS and SERVICE

Arizona
SCOTTSDALE
Cavallino Classics
(602) 991-5322

California
HOLLYWOOD
Hollywood Sport Cars
(213) 464-6161

LOS GATOS
Ferrari of Los Gatos
(408) 354-4000

NEWPORT BEACH
Newport Imports
(714) 722-4100

SAN DIEGO
Cornes Motors
(619) 578-8600

SAN FRANCISCO
R & R Classic Cars
(415) 474-8000

SEASIDE
Monterey Ferrari
(408) 899-8800

WALNUT CREEK
Walnut Creek Ferrari
(415) 947-1800

WOODLAND HILLS
Ogner Motorcars
(818) 884-4411

Colorado
LAKEWOOD
Roger Mauro Imports
(303) 233-3336

Connecticut
GREENWICH
Miller Motorcars
(203) 629-3890

Florida
CORAL GABLES
Ferrari Collection
(305) 444-5555

FORT LAUDERDALE
Shelton Sports Cars
(305) 493-5211

ST. PETERSBURG
Crown Auto Dealerships
(813) 527-5731

Georgia
TUCKER
F.A.F. Motorcars
(404) 939-5464

Hawaii
HONOLULU
Continental Cars
(808) 537-5365

Illinois
HINSDALE
Continental Motors
(708) 655-3535

LAKE FOREST
Lake Forest Sportscars
(708) 295-6560

Kansas
SHAWNEE MISSION
Aristocrat Motor Company
(913) 677-3300

Massachusetts
COHASSET
Autohaus
(617) 383-0095

FRAMINGHAM
Gaston Andrey of Framingham
(508) 875-0639

Michigan
DEARBORN
The Sports Car Exchange
(313) 581-6222

Mississippi
JACKSON
Ferrari South
(601) 969-5668

Missouri
RICHMOND HEIGHTS
Brentwood Ferrari
(314) 862-9501

New York
GREAT NECK
Auto Torino
(516) 829-6020

NEW YORK CITY
Steven Kessler Motor Cars
(212) 689-0770

SPRING VALLEY
Wide World of Cars
(914) 425-2600

North Carolina
GREENSBORO
Foreign Cars Italia
(919) 852-2158

Ohio
DUBLIN
Midwestern Auto Group
(614) 889-2571

Oklahoma
NORMAN
Big Red Sports/Imports
(405) 364-4400

Oregon
PORTLAND
Ron Tonkin Gran Turismo
(503) 255-7560

Pennsylvania
ROSEMONT
Algar Enterprises
(215) 527-1100

Rhode Island
MIDDLETOWN
Ferrari of Newport
(401) 849-2500

Tennessee
NASHVILLE
Thoroughbred Motorcars
(615) 385-1900

Texas
HOUSTON
Ferrari of Houston
(713) 772-3868

DALLAS
Classic Ferrari
(214) 470-9410

SAN ANTONIO
Motor Imports
(512) 341-2800

Utah
SALT LAKE CITY
Steve Harris Imports
(801) 521-0340

Virginia
ARLINGTON
American Service Center
(703) 525-2100

Washington
SEATTLE
Grand Prix Motors
(206) 329-7070

Canada

British Columbia
VANCOUVER
Carter Motor Cars
(604) 736-2821

Ontario
TORONTO
G.L. Automobiles
(416) 535-9900

WOODBRIDGE
Maranello Sports Cars
(416) 749-5325

Quebec
VILLE ST.-LAURENT
Luigi Sports Car
(514) 336-4449